DATE DUE

DATE DUE			
AUG 1 0 '88			

Naturalistic Triptych:

The Fictive and the Real in Zola, Mann, and Dreiser

Naturalistic Triptych:
The Fictive and the Real in Zola, Mann, and Dreiser

Haskell M. Block

Random House   New York

On the cover: Acknowledgment is made to Marc Bernard
and Editions du Seuil for the photograph of the Duboutin
drawing of Emile Zola; to the Konservator, Thomas
Mann-Archiv, Eidg. Technische Hochschule for the photograph
of Thomas Mann; and to Lotte Jacobi for the photograph
of Theodore Dreiser, Copyright by Lotte Jacobi,
Hillsboro, New Hampshire.

For Elaine

Preface

The study of the fictive and the real in the naturalistic novel is essentially a study of how naturalistic novels were made and of the relationship of their authors' theoretical premises to the novels as completed works of art. It seemed preferable to limit the discussion to detailed consideration of three major naturalistic novels, rather than to attempt a broad survey of the naturalistic novel in all of its manifestations. The three novels selected for examination are, I hope, sufficiently representative to provide a basis for at least tentative generalizations concerning the character of naturalistic fictional art. The consideration of the interplay of the fictive and the real should help to illuminate both the uniqueness of the individual novels and their common naturalistic elements and to clarify the role of naturalism as a broad international current and style of modern literature.

Any scholarly and critical enterprise is perforce a collaborative undertaking. This study would not have been possible without the contributions of many others. Specific obligations are indicated in the notes to each chapter, but I am deeply conscious of my large and abiding indebtedness to teachers, colleagues, students, and others, living and dead.

I am grateful to the Random House staff for assistance of every kind. I especially appreciate the helpful collaboration of Estelle Fine, Carol Green, and Claire Adams, who edited the manuscript and prepared it for publication.

The writing of this study was stimulated by the meeting at

Strasbourg, France, of the Tenth Congress of the International Federation for Modern Languages and Literatures (September 1966).

I have translated all of the foreign language quotations in the text. All page references and notes are to the editions listed in the bibliography. As for the title, it is hoped that the side panels set the center piece in relief and that all three panels are hinged together.

H. M. B.

Contents

Naturalistic Triptych:

The Fictive and the Real in
Zola, Mann, and Dreiser

1
Introduction: The Problem of Naturalism

Naturalism, like all generalizations which serve to order and classify literature, is a most difficult term to define with absolute precision. Its vagueness is inherent in the very attempt to impose a broad unifying concept on so seemingly free and diverse an activity as literary creation. The labels devised by both writers and readers to clarify the meaning of literature often give rise to as much confusion as clarification, but the widespread use of such terms and their enormous impact on both the making and the understanding of literature testify to their real importance. Like classicism, Romanticism, and realism, naturalism has served to emphasize common elements of individual works and to blur their differences, yet these common elements are not hypothetical but correspond to qualities actually present in the works themselves. The term "naturalism" as applied to the modern novel would not have lasted for almost a century if it did not in fact help define and illuminate some of the general characteristics of the modern novel as well as the salient attributes of specific novels. In the course of its usage, naturalism has been defined and redefined so many times that perhaps it would be more accurate to speak of "naturalisms" rather than naturalism, to indicate the multiplicity of meanings expressed in a single term. Most writers and readers, however, are less demanding in such matters than historians of ideas or of literature.

Rather than discard the term because of its ambiguities, we should try to use it with what precision it will allow, recognizing that such broad classifications can never adequately define the complexities of literary art.

Naturalism has been most commonly described as either a literary group or school, a literary movement or period, a way of looking at literature and life, a method for the creation of literary works, or a literary technique and style. These descriptions are not mutually exclusive, nor do they constitute a complete list. Some students of naturalism see it as an intensified and exaggerated mode of realism, thereby shifting but not resolving the problem of definition. Still others have insisted that naturalism, in expression if not in theory, is a mode of Romanticism. For most students of the modern novel, however, naturalism, with all its ambiguities, is distinct from both Romanticism and realism. When used to designate a group of writers, naturalism commonly refers to Emile Zola and his followers; Zola, however, insisted that he did not invent the term and denied that there was a naturalistic *cénacle,* or school. To speak of a naturalistic movement or period, extending perhaps from 1870 to 1900, is to simplify unduly the variety of conflicting and contradictory assumptions and norms that prevailed during the closing decades of the past century. In its historical context, naturalism was but one of many literary tendencies of the day. As an attitude, naturalism may be considered a constant element in human experience, free of dependence on any particular time and place, and asserting a view of both art and life that may be held not only by writers but by anyone. As a method, naturalism is generally regarded as an instrument and a procedure derived from the natural sciences and applied to literature. It is in this sense that Zola usually employs the term. Finally, as a literary technique or style, naturalism may be viewed as a distinct way of ordering the elements of an art form. In this sense, the term has been used by literary critics and historians to characterize individual novels and to group under a common classification novelists embodying the specific qualities ascribed to naturalistic art. On occasion, such groupings have led to the formulation of naturalism as a "period style" or as a literary current or tradition that is present in several literatures but is discontinuous in its manifestations. The usual definition of naturalism employed today is still that provided by Zola himself, for it was as a direct result of Zola's own efforts both as theorist and novelist that the concept of naturalism came to be generally adopted as a literary term.

Any approach to the critical study of the naturalistic novel must therefore begin with Zola. This is not to say that Zola's definition of naturalism will describe any and all naturalistic novels, whether by Zola himself or by novelists who responded to his program. Yet, if we are to view naturalism in a broad perspective, we must recognize Zola's enormous impact. Despite his insistence that naturalism was neither new nor limited to his own theory and expression, as a literary technique and style it is essentially Zola's invention; its widespread emulation and acceptance in Zola's time and in our own is a tribute not only to the power of his art but also to the force of his incessant propaganda on behalf of the new impulse.

The term "naturalism" had a long history before Zola made it into a battle cry.[1] Generally, it had been used to indicate any materialistic, secular, or scientific attitude toward human experience. In the middle years of the nineteenth century in France, "naturalist" was a synonym for natural scientist, but it was also used to describe writers whose procedures resembled those of the scientist. Early in his career, well before he was recognized as a novelist, Zola praised the positivist critic Taine as "a naturalist philosopher who declares that the intellectual world is subject to laws in the same way as the material world." [2] Taine had called special attention to the similarity of Balzac's methods in his novels and those of scientific naturalists. Zola repeatedly employed the term "naturalistic" in this sense in his journalistic articles as early as 1866, long before the appearance of his manifesto of naturalism, *Le Roman expérimental* (*The Experimental Novel*), in 1880. Indeed, both the term and the program which it embodies are clearly set forth by Zola in his preface to the second edition of his novel *Thérèse Raquin*

(1868). The preface is a polemical reply to those who assailed the novel as "Putrid Literature"; it indicates unmistakably that Zola's essential convictions were formulated some years before he read Claude Bernard's account of the experimental method, on which *Le Roman expérimental* is based. In writing *Thérèse Raquin,* Zola insists, "my aim was above all a scientific one." Each chapter, he contends, is the study of "a curious physiological case." The novelist's cold and objective analysis of passion is viewed by Zola as exactly the same as "the analytical work which surgeons perform on cadavers." For Zola, the strength, boldness, and violence of his novel are all in keeping with its fidelity to experience. In the final lines of his preface he declares: "The group of naturalist writers to which I have the honor to belong has enough courage and energy to produce strong works, which will carry their own defense."

Sympathetic readers of *Thérèse Raquin,* such as Taine, admired the novel for its convincing analysis of physiological and psychological forces, but Taine urged Zola to cast a wider net in his subsequent novels and to take Balzac and Shakespeare as his models. Undoubtedly, Taine played an important part in helping Zola to plan the great design of the *Rougon-Macquart* series of novels as a mirror of a whole society. Clearly inspired by Balzac's gigantic conception of *La Comédie humaine,* Zola's *Rougon-Macquart* is grandiosely subtitled "A Natural and Social History of a Family during the Second Empire." Yet, for some time before the conception of this vast project, Zola had seen his approach to reality as somewhat different from that of Balzac—in his more acute awareness of the coercive force of heredity and environment. To the influence of milieu, derived chiefly from Balzac and Taine, Zola added the rigorous determinism of the laws of heredity as proclaimed by the biologists of the day. In the preface to *Thérèse Raquin,* he describes his central figures as "human beasts," totally devoid of free will, "dragged along each act of their life by the fatalities of their flesh." From the beginning of his theoretical formulations, the analogy between the novelist and the scientist and the insistence on a thoroughgoing biological and social determinism in human events are the foundations of Zola's naturalism.

Zola's collection of essays *Le Roman expérimental* is by far the best known statement of his doctrines. His most ambitious formulations occur in the title essay, a polemical document which is not as measured or as carefully qualified in its assertions as some of the other essays in the collection. Precisely because of its extreme and categorical claims, the essay entitled "The Experimental Novel" is one of Zola's weakest theoretical statements, yet its programmatic definition of naturalism is primarily responsible for the way the term has been understood by most readers since Zola's time. The experimental novel, he contends, is "the literature of our scientific age." The novelist must employ the same methods as the scientist if his novels are to constitute a truthful representation of life:

> In a word, we must operate on characters, passions, human and social events, as the chemist and physician operate on brute matter, as the physiologist operates on living beings. Determinism dominates everything. It is scientific investigation, it is experimental reasoning, which combats one by one the hypotheses of idealists, and which replaces the novels of pure imagination by novels of observation and experimentation. (p. 23)

Repeatedly in this essay, Zola insists that naturalism is neither a school nor an activity of a particular writer or group; it consists solely of "the application of the experimental method to the study of nature and man." The method is everything, and, as a method, Zola believes that naturalism will come to dominate all literature. It should be noted that Zola explicitly states that naturalism is not a form, a style, or a technique. These will follow from the method, which implies for Zola not only an attitude and a perspective but also a distinct mode of procedure in fictional composition.

In *Le Roman expérimental* Zola does not seem to regard naturalism as a literary movement, but in the polemical essays which he wrote soon afterward he fuses the notions of a method and a movement. In an essay entitled "Naturalism," included in the collection *Une Campagne* (*A Campaign,* 1882), he writes of naturalism as the third great movement of French literature, after classicism and Romanticism. The first period of the nineteenth century, he asserts, was dominated by Romanticism; the second period will be that of naturalism. Here, naturalism is plainly defined as a historical movement as well as a literary method. Zola's introduction of a historical concept is unquestionably one of the principal sources of confusion in the definition of naturalism which has prevailed since his time. Proof of the persistence of this confusion in our own day may be found in almost any of the standard handbooks and dictionaries of literary terms.

As a result of Zola's five volumes of criticism proclaiming the ascendency of naturalism in the novel, the term came into vogue almost at once. Unquestionably, the growing success of Zola's novels, particularly after the publication of *L'Assommoir* in 1877, helped to attract attention to his theories. By the time he wrote *Le Roman expérimental,* he was an experienced and a successful novelist, and there is perhaps more than a little malice in Edmond de Goncourt's account of Zola's alleged declaration that naturalism was nothing more than a way of calling attention to his work and of promoting his literary career.[3] As we have seen, the main elements of Zola's naturalistic theory were completely formulated a decade before 1878, the year in which he first came to know Claude Bernard's *Introduction to the Study of Experimental Medicine.* Despite the extreme character of Zola's theories in "The Experimental Novel," there can be no doubt of his solidity of conviction and seriousness of purpose.

Nevertheless, it has not been difficult for readers in either Zola's time or our own to point to contradictions in his theories. These contradictions are in fact expressions of tensions in his mind and art which are all but submerged in the manifesto in which he proclaims the experimental method. In an essay of 1881, restating a formula expressed fifteen years earlier, Zola defines a literary work as "a corner of nature seen through a temperament." In this recognition of the role of the artist's temperament in literary creation, he implicitly repudiates any reduction of art to photography or to a mechanical transcription of external reality. Even in "The Experimental Novel," he insists on the importance of genius and the modifying power of selection in the application of the experimental method. In subsequent essays, he goes further, declaring that the canon of value of a literary creation is not its accuracy of representation, but rather the grandeur of the spectacle of nature, the intensity of the writer's view of reality: "the powerful way he deforms it to make it fit into his mould, the imprint he leaves on all he touches, this is real creation, the true sign of genius." [4] Clearly, if we look beyond "The Experimental Novel" to Zola's letters and his later critical essays, we shall find that his definition of naturalism is not as wooden and as mechanical as has frequently been contended.

A similar inconsistency can be seen in juxtaposing Zola's novels and his doctrines. His works reflect not only his scientific and sociological preoccupations but also his exuberant fantasy and his penchant for extraordinary incidents that issue in violent drama and colossal symbolic configurations. As his American follower Frank Norris points out, the citation of Zola as a realist is "a strange perversion." Basing his account of naturalism on Zola's novels rather than on the theories of "The Experimental Novel," Norris asserts:

> The naturalist takes no note of common people, common in so far as their interests, their lives, and the things that occur in them are common, are ordinary. Terrible things must happen to the characters of the naturalistic tale. They must be twisted from the ordinary, wrenched out from the quiet, uneventful round of every-day life, and flung into the throes of a vast and terrible drama that works itself out in unleashed passions, in blood, and in sudden death.[5]

Zola himself was acutely aware of the large distance between the theories of "The Experimental Novel" and his boldly imaginative art. As he remarks in a letter of December 28, 1882: "It is certain that I am a poet and that my works are built like great musical symphonies. . . . I am steeped in romanticism up to my waist." The definition of naturalism which emerges from Zola's novels is at such variance with his programmatic doctrines that some readers have contended that his theories are altogether irrelevant to his novels. This, too, may be an extreme position. On the whole, Zola was a rather good critic with a keen awareness of the theoretical bases of his art. It is nonetheless evident that the problem of defining naturalism and of describing the salient characteristics of naturalistic novels has been rendered more difficult by the wide gap separating the doctrines of "The Experimental Novel" from the art of Zola's fiction.

The expansion of the subject matter of the novel in France was accomplished as much by Zola's predecessors, notably Balzac and Flaubert, as by Zola himself. Yet because of the fullness of detail with which Zola, in some of his novels, depicts scenes of depravity and vice, particularly among characters drawn from the lower classes, naturalism for many readers came to be associated with sordid and brutal events and "low" characters. In vain did Zola protest that naturalism as a method could be applied to any subject and to any plane of society. For most readers, naturalistic fiction was defined not only by its embodiment of deterministic laws of nature but also by its portrayal of harsh events and crude characters. Thus, in an essay entitled "The New Naturalism" in *The Fortnightly Review* in 1885, W. S. Lilly declares that "the results obtainable by his [Zola's] researches in the latrine and brothel are of precisely the same value as those which the vivisector derives from the torture trough." It is difficult for readers today to understand the almost pathological reactions of anger and disgust aroused by naturalistic novels at the end of the past century. In claiming all of life as their province, Zola and his followers merely intensified a development in the novel that was well under way before Zola's proclamation of his credo. The naturalists provided not so much a new subject matter as a new emphasis on areas of experience which had been ignored if not repudiated by most earlier novelists. For Zola himself, the enlargement of subject matter was simply a necessary part of the novelist's responsibility to the social and natural forces of his time. The novel as the naturalists conceived it is not a mode of casual amusement but an instrument for the discovery of truth.

In the essays which constitute *Le Roman expérimental,* as well as in his conversations with young writers and interviews with journalists, Zola describes at great length the process by which he felt the naturalistic novelist arrives at truth in art.[6] In keeping with the analogy of the novelist and the scientist, the novel as a controlled experiment must be based on observation. The novelist's point of departure and the "solid terrain" of his characters and events are the observer's "facts as he has observed them." This observation must be thorough, impartial, and exact if the novel is to be a truthful representation of experience. For the naturalistic novelist, Zola insists, observation is the indispensable starting point of fictional creation.

The result of the method which Zola set forth for the composition of a naturalistic novel is to make the fictive almost completely dependent on the real. The fidelity to experience of the novel is based above all on the novelist's documentation of his characters and their milieu. Clearly, Zola views the process of documentation as crucial, not only in his own art but in that of any novelist who would adopt the naturalistic method. The process is most fully described in an essay entitled "Le Sens du Réel" ("The Sense of the Real"), included in *Le Roman expérimental.* In the naturalistic novel, Zola says, the romantic assertion of the imagination is suppressed: "All the efforts of the writer tend to conceal the imaginary beneath the real." He does not claim that the imagination is totally absent in the new novel, but rather that the sense of the real is achieved essentially through documentation, in a process which he describes in some detail:

It would be a curious study to describe how our great contemporary novelists work. They base almost all of their works on notes, taken at great length. When they have studied with scrupulous care the terrain on which they are to move, when they have investigated all the sources and have in hand the many documents they need, only then do they decide to write. The plan of the work is given them by the documents themselves, for it happens that facts classify themselves logically, this one before that. A symmetry is established, the story composes itself out of all the collected observations, all the notes, one leading to another by the very enchainment of the life of the characters, and the conclusion is nothing more than a natural and inevitable consequence. (p. 166)

Thus, documentation furnishes the materials of art; the author need only attend to their disposition. Zola also admits, however, that the novelist's use of his materials is by no means as automatic as this preoccupation with factual investigation would suggest. At the very end of his essay, he recognizes that, in the work of a truly significant novelist, the sense of the real must be accompanied by the power of personal expression: "A great novelist, in our time, is one who has the sense of the real and who expresses nature with originality, by making it live with its own life." In insisting on the necessity for the novelist to create an autonomous and independent world, Zola moves beyond his earlier assertion of the total dependence of the fictive on the real.

Despite his recognition that documentation alone is insufficient to produce great art, Zola's elaborate account of his own processes of composition helps to explain why, for many of his readers, naturalistic fiction is defined as the depiction of sordid events based on painstaking documentation. It is precisely in this sense that Henry James, who knew Zola's work well and responded to it with grudging admiration, describes, in a letter of December 12, 1884, his preparations for the writing of a prison scene in *The Princess Casamassima:*

I have been all the morning at Millbank prison (horrible place) collecting notes for a fiction scene. You see I am quite the Naturalist. Look out for the same—a year hence.[7]

James could hardly be described as a naturalistic novelist, but it is important to note that naturalistic methods and values enter into the work of many novelists whose art is in most respects quite remote from that of Zola. Clearly, for James, documentation is only a phase of fictional creation, a way of making the novel a more convincing and lifelike work of art; but this may also be the case for more naturalistic novelists as well. The main difference in this respect might only be one of emphasis. Presumably, documentation is more vital to the naturalist and consequently more detailed so as to underscore the requisite sense of fact. A further and more important difference between naturalistic novels and others lies in the enchainment of material circumstances in the naturalistic novel, demonstrating the deterministic role of natural and environmental forces in the movement of events.

Like so many of Zola's premises, determinism in the naturalistic novel turns out to be more of a tendency than a dogma. As Zola's *L'Assommoir* clearly illustrates, accident may play a crucial role in the relentless movement toward catastrophe in the novel. The tensions of freedom and determinism in the naturalistic novel are analogous to the conflicting claims of the fictive and the real. These tensions seem to be particularly marked in American naturalistic novels, but they may also characterize the works of Zola and of his European followers as well. No naturalistic novelist seems to have written in absolute accord with the doctrines set forth by Zola in his manifesto. If we adopt Zola's definition, all naturalistic novelists, including Zola himself, are impure. Despite the contentions of some of Zola's doctrinaire followers, there are no "consistent naturalists" whose works are of high artistic value.

When we direct our attention to the study of particular novels composed, at least to some extent, under the impact of naturalistic theories, we are confronted with an immense range of individual differences, depending, as Zola himself admitted, on the temperament of the novelist and on the distinct combination of artistic elements in his work, elements on occasion totally unrelated to or even at variance with naturalism. Nevertheless, all naturalistic novelists share with Zola a recognition that some dependence on the literal and the actual is indispensable if the novel is to represent a cross section of life with the requisite degree of verisimilitude. It is therefore no surprise to find in the composition of representative naturalistic novels a considerable reliance on factual documentation, often based on the personal experience of the novelist but also on his use of oral and written sources. The importance of these sources, however, should not be overemphasized. Of primary significance in the making of a novel—or of any work of art—is not the mere existence of specific sources but their transformation into art. If this transformation does not take place in the act of composition, the work itself remains only a document, devoid of aesthetic value. The situation of the naturalistic novelist in his deliberate closeness to actuality may be extreme, yet the problem of the assimilation and transformation of life into art may ultimately prove to be no different for him than for other novelists.

The problem of defining naturalism cannot be resolved as long as we insist on a rigorous conformity to the theories set forth in "The Experimental Novel." A useful definition must be based on the novels themselves as well as on the novelist's theoretical assumptions. Indeed, the latter are important only insofar as they are actually embodied in works of art. If naturalism represents not only an attitude but also a literary tradition and style, it should be possible to discover common devices and techniques in particular naturalistic novels, as well as common underlying assumptions and processes of composition. For the student of literature who is concerned with broad historical and stylistic trends, it is of some importance to determine to what extent naturalistic novels reflect essential similarities in the transformation of the real into the fictive and in the interplay of these dimensions. Any generalization is bound to be limited by the examples on which it rests, but the examples need not be arbitrary, even if they cannot be exhaustive. The three novels selected for analysis in this study—Zola's *L'Assommoir,* Mann's *Buddenbrooks,* and Dreiser's *An American Tragedy*—are all to some degree naturalistic novels and offer common ground for the elucidation of principles and methods of composition. These particular novels have been selected for discussion partly because of the considerable recognition they have received as literary works of a high order of excellence and also because, through the efforts of scholarship, we have access to sufficient documentary source material for each novel to enable us to study both the writer's dependence on his documentation and his modification of it. The interaction of the fictive and the real is only one aspect of the naturalistic novel, but it is of central importance, and its study in the context of concrete artistic expression may help to point the way to a redefinition of literary naturalism.

II
Zola's *L'Assommoir*

Zola's *L'Assommoir* (1877) is considered by many to be his best novel. For purposes of our study, we fortunately know a great deal about his plans for the novel and the process of its composition.[1] As early as 1869, Zola noted the plan of a *roman ouvrier* as part of the general outline of the emerging Rougon-Macquart series. As he later said in the preface to *L'Assommoir*: "I wished to depict the fatal decay of a working-class family, in the foul milieu of our industrial suburbs." The purposeful documentation for the novel began late in 1875, after Zola had sketched out the *ébauche,* or outline, indicating the sequence of chapters and the traits of the principal characters.[2] For some years, he had been absorbing details of the daily life of the working classes, beginning with his own impoverished early residence in Paris in 1860 and 1861, when he had sometimes gone for days with virtually nothing to eat. From his daily association with the poor, he knew well the ravages caused by broken families, alcoholism, debauchery, and disease. This direct familiarity was reinforced by careful and elaborate documentation; he had evidently begun collecting newspaper reports for a working class novel as early as 1868. Thus, the brutal episode of the suffering and death of little Lalie Bijard at the hands of her intoxicated and sadistic father was drawn in both outline and details from an article published by Louis Ratisbonne in the journal *L'Evénement.* Zola also noted and preserved for later use a descriptive account of the daily life of the working class by Francisque Sarcey entitled "A Wolff et à Richard," published in *Le Gaulois* in February 1870.[3] From both of these articles Zola subsequently incorporated sentences almost verbatim into his novel, but their primary function was to indicate a tone and a direction of treatment of the milieu as well as to provide specific details. Against the background of his early experiences and his dossier of newspaper articles, Zola set out deliberately to steep himself in the milieu, so as to produce, as he noted in the outline, "a most exact tableau of the life of the masses." Thus, he said to Paul Alexis in a letter of October 20, 1875: "from the day after my arrival, I have to open the campaign for my novel, find a section of the city, visit the workers." His preparations led him not only to a particular neighborhood but also to long visits to sections of the city that were to figure in the novel: the laundry, the bistro, the forge, the workshop of a gold chain maker, the restaurants and dance halls, the shops and the streets. He even drew up a map of the *quartier* and a plan of the house on the Rue de la Goutte d'Or, where most of the novel takes place. Despite his attention to details, Zola's visual observation was probably rapid and highly selective and was supplemented considerably by his reliance on personal experience and written sources.[4] Some of the details of the life of the working classes in the novel were taken from an essay published in 1870 by Denis Poulot entitled "Question sociale: Le Sublime ou le Travailleur, comme il est en 1870 et ce qu'il peut être" ("A Social Question: The Sublime or the Laborer, as he is in 1870 and as he might be"), and occasional passages from Poulot are repeated almost word for word in *L'Assommoir*.[5] *"Le Sublime"* is Poulot's ironic term for the shiftless worker: "lazy, violent, and drunk." It must be noted, however, that Zola's borrowings from Poulot constitute a very small part of the novel as a whole. For the account in the final chapter of the death of Coupeau from delirium tremens, Zola relied in large part on a study of alcoholism and its physiological effects by Dr. Valentin Magnan, and for the language of the novel he supplemented his knowledge of working-class argot by studying Delvau's *Dictionnaire de la langue verte* and similar manuals, from which he compiled a vocabulary list. When we recall that the serialized text of the novel published in *Le Bien Public* in 1876 bore the subtitle, subsequently dropped, of *Roman de mœurs parisiennes* (*A*

Novel of Parisian Manners), we can appreciate the psychological importance for Zola himself of his immersion in his milieu; this saturation process provided him with the sureness of command of his subject necessary for fluid and massive composition. Zola's own emphasis on the importance of documentation testifies to the acuteness of his need for this assurance; yet the study of the relationship of source material to the novel seems to suggest that Zola, as well as his early disciples and critics, greatly overstressed its importance.

Zola's researches into the milieu were directed not simply to the milieu as object but to the role of the milieu as an explanation of the behavior of his characters. The intrigue of *L'Assommoir* is built solidly around the figure of Gervaise, whose life in Paris provides the chronological framework of events. In her relationships to Lantier, Coupeau, and Goujet, Zola develops a highly elaborate and complex plot, but also an orderly one, for the relentless process of physical and moral decay gives shape and direction to the immense panorama of action. He charts the crucial stages in the life of Gervaise through a series of sharply defined scenes or tableaux, such as the *bataille du lavoir,* the wedding scene, the *fête,* as well as through more intimate portrayals of her private life. The scenic method, the sweep and flow of the narrative, and the solidity of characterization depend far more on Zola's art than on his documentation. As Henri Massis comments by way of conclusion to his study of the making of *L'Assommoir:* "*Even though he had sufficient documentation, Zola invented much more than he observed.*" [6]

Zola may have viewed Gervaise as a symbol of her class, who is entrapped, punished, and finally reduced to squalor and a miserable death, a victim of a malign determinism. Nevertheless, it is the vividness and immediacy of Zola's characterization that renders her unique as she struggles for a time heroically to overcome the limits of her environment and fails as much in consequence of Coupeau's accident as through her own weakness. The *ménage à trois,* which Zola considered the turning point of the plot, is itself a result of the accident and of Coupeau's subsequent degradation. Yet Gervaise is not a wholly passive victim of circumstance. As Zola noted in his outline, she is a woman who has suffered considerably even in her youth and who is nonetheless willing and able to face the demands of life, "ready by nature to fight back and to work." And Zola adds: "to sum it up, quite *sympathique*." Our sympathy for Gervaise reflects Zola's deep compassion for her suffering, even as he portrays her reduction to begging and prostitution. Her death is quiet and simple after Coupeau's long delirium, but it is no less sordid, for although Coupeau ends as a case study at Saint-Anne, Gervaise ends deprived even of her modest wish, "to die in her own bed." As Jacques Dubois has strikingly demonstrated, the process of Gervaise's decay is charted by her successive residences; her quest for a refuge is the source of an intricate configuration of images and symbols. Her death is poignant as well as ironic, and places in clear perspective both the nobility and the wretchedness of her existence. She emerges in the round as a fully created character. In the depiction of Gervaise, the fictive values of Zola's art at once embody and transcend the plane of the real.

The heroic efforts of Gervaise in the early chapters of the novel to surmount the limitations of her circumstances and milieu lend her a dignity and stature which intensifies the pathos of her subsequent decay. Zola presents her fully individualized, perhaps more so than any of his other characters in the vast body of his work. We should recall that the original title of *L'Assommoir* was *La Simple Vie de Gervaise Macquart*. Despite her symbolic function, Gervaise is not a statistic or a case study but a warm and courageous human being. In a subsequent comment on his heroine, Zola remarked: "she remains good to the end." [7] This goodness and dignity is brought out in the first elaborate scene of the novel, the *bataille du lavoir*. Aware of the dangers of flatness and monotony in the mere description of the daily life of his heroine, Zola noted in his *ébauche* the need to dramatize her character and situation in the scene in the *lavoir*. He confided to Edmondo de Amicis his conviction that the account of the public laundry was absolutely authentic: "It is the description of a real laundry, where I spent long hours." Yet this description is only a background to the human drama. The readiness of Gervaise to fight in defense of her honor and good name and to lash out at the meanness around her enlists our admiration. Far from constituting an *hors d'œuvre* outside of the intrigue of the novel, the fight defines Gervaise's character and introduces the motif of her struggle for survival. In *Confessions of a Young Man,* George Moore has sensitively described Zola's "immense harmonic development":

> . . . the fight motive is indicated, then follows the develop-
> ment of side issues, then comes the fight motive explained; it
> is broken off short, it flutters through a web of progressive de-
> tail, the fight motive is again taken up, and now it is worked
> out in all its fulness; it is worked up to *crescendo,* another
> issue is introduced, and again the theme is given forth.

This intricate interplay of themes is remote indeed from photographic realism. Gervaise's struggle against poverty and moral degradation is on the very point of success when Coupeau's accident ensues. Even then, she fights back valiantly and, for a time, successfully. It is the decay of Coupeau which drags Gervaise along, for she is not strong enough to resist Lantier indefinitely. Despite her marriage, her love for Lantier has not wholly vanished, but her feelings are at first controlled by her loyalty and affection for Coupeau. Her sexual surrender to Lantier occurs under circumstances that render it understandable and not altogether culpable, despite her earlier vow to Goujet not to yield, for her fall takes place in a moment of deep revulsion over Coupeau's drunkenness and filth. Nevertheless, Gervaise must bear the responsibility for her weakness, and she pays dearly for it. The *ménage à trois* is at the base of the ruin of the family; Coupeau and Lantier drink while Gervaise works, and her economic and moral decay proceeds relentlessly. Reduced to an animal-like existence, exhausted by her menial work, surrounded by suffering and depravity on every side, she still retains a shred of dignity, as in her consciousness of humiliation when she goes to beg from the Lorilleux. Even to the bitter moments of her end, Gervaise's personal destiny engages us; we share Zola's admiration for her courage and his pity for her misery.

Unquestionably, Zola's careful observation of the circumstances and milieu of his heroine helped him to render her with deep understanding. The solid groundwork of reality animates the fictive creation of character. Many sympathetic readers fail to give full recognition to the fusion of reality and poetic vision in Zola's art of characterization. Angus Wilson is perhaps unique in describing Gervaise as the most completely conceived character drawn from the class of the very poor in the whole of nineteenth-century fiction. Flaubert's admiring praise of the depiction of Nana in a letter of February 15, 1880, "Nana turns to myth, without ceasing to be real," can surely be said of Gervaise as well. Her suffering and defeat embody at once a personal and a symbolic destiny. Zola's documentation no doubt helped him to portray his heroine with concreteness and immediacy, but the compassion and sympathy she evokes in the course of her hopeless struggle are essentially the work of the novelist. The direction and control of the reader's responses express the primacy of the fictive rather than the real in Zola's art.

Zola's presentation of his minor characters seems to reveal relatively little dependence on specific documentation. As we might suppose, several of them are drawn, at least in part, after people he knew. Thus, Lantier resembles a certain Coupin, Lorilleux a certain Kretz, and Mme Poisson is drawn after Mme Kretz. In a discussion of the dramatic adaptation of *L'Assommoir,* Zola declares: "In real life, I knew many Coupeaus, slowly stupefied by drink," but he indicates no single model, and there may not have been any. Some of the most striking characters, such as Père Bazouge, seem to be figures of pure invention.[8] Although some of the names and traits of Coupeau's drinking companions were carried over from Poulot's *Le Sublime,* as were the essential qualities of Goujet, Zola's documentary source offers only a few broad and general indications. In his plan for the novel, he notes, apropos of the virtuous blacksmith, "the true worker" (see *Sublime*). The "true worker," according to Poulot, never contracts debts, saves his money, respects women, children, and the aged, buys books, studies, never gets drunk, rests on Sunday, and respects his employer. Goujet's character may have been suggested by Poulot, but the function of the blacksmith in the narrative is solely Zola's contribution. Subsequently, he felt that he may have falsified the depiction of Goujet, "for I have lent him feelings that are not those of his milieu";[9] but this would also be true for Gervaise, at least during the first half of the novel. There may have been other grounds for Zola's dissatisfaction with his treatment of Goujet. In the initial planning of the scenario, the novel was to culminate in violence and melodrama, with Gervaise attempting to throw acid at Lantier and Virginie, and with Coupeau, Lantier, and Goujet subsequently engaging in a three-cornered brawl with knives.[10] Zola wisely substituted a simpler and more restrained ending, but perhaps the death of Coupeau remains as a concession to his earlier theatrical plan. Goujet virtually recedes from the novel as the pace of Gervaise's downward journey accelerates, yet one cannot help feeling that Zola planned to use the blacksmith in a more functional and a more sustained role. The ideal love which Goujet represents for Gervaise is more evident in the theatrical adaptation of L'Assommoir by Busnach and Gastineau, which ends with Gervaise confessing in her last moments: "Listen, monsieur Goujet, now I can tell you. I won't trouble anyone any more . . . I have always loved you! (*She dies*)." Whereupon Goujet exclaims: "Poor creature!" Goujet, like all of the minor figures in the novel, is relatively flat, but on the whole Zola is remarkably skillful in enlivening his secondary characters. Thus, Mes-Bottes with his dozen loaves of bread each meal, Mme Lerat with her off-color suggestiveness, Bazouge with his private brand of philosophical consolation, Poisson with his imperturbable sense of order, Clémence with her indifferent gross sensuality—these and countless others support the rich and full delineation of milieu and often lend humor and comic relief to the harsh and brutal narrative.

In his approach to milieu as well as to character, Zola at his best does not write in the manner of a scientist who makes his clinical observations with objectivity and detachment; rather, he humanizes his characters and their environment. The milieu in the novel is functional, not inert, and frequently it takes on a symbolic dimension through Zola's art of metaphorical enlargement. Nowhere is this symbolizing process more evident than in the expansion of Père Colombe's distillation apparatus seen through the eyes of Gervaise. Zola's scenario for the novel contains the bare notation: *"L'Assommoir* with the machine and its details. The machine makes Gervaise cold with fear." Our first view of the apparatus comes early in the novel, on the occasion of Gervaise's first visit to Père Colombe's in the company of Coupeau. Although Zola's initial brief description is almost wholly objective, it prepares us subtly for the symbolic enlargement at the end of Gervaise's visit, as she stands horrified and bewildered by the enormity and complexity of the machine:

> The still, with its queerly shaped receptacles, its endless coils of pipe, maintained a somber appearance; not a wisp of smoke escaped from it; you could barely hear a breathing inside of it, a subterranean snoring; it was like a dark deed performed in open day by a grim workman, powerful and silent. (p. 51)

Zola invests the machine with mystery and terror and with organic, animate existence. Pictorial realism gives place to vivid imaginative elaboration. The symbolic enlargement proceeds almost at once, as a frame to the movements and reactions of Coupeau and Gervaise:

> The still dumbly continued to work, letting flow its sweat of alcohol like a slow and stubborn fountain, which would finally invade the room, flow out on to the outer boulevards, inundate the immense expanse of Paris. (p. 52)

The distillation apparatus, metamorphosed into a man-devouring monster, looms larger than the city itself. What Armand Lanoux has called Zola's "anthropomorphic amplification" gives dynamic utterance to the fear and demoralization of his heroine. The littleness of the terrified beholder and her inability to surmount the oppressive force of her milieu are underscored by Zola's striking contrast of the simplicity and terror of Gervaise and the intricate, impassive, and overpowering machine, a symbol not only of the fury wrought by alcohol but of the complex and overwhelming pressure of her surroundings and daily life as well. After Coupeau's return from his first attack of delirium tremens, Gervaise finds him in a drunken stupor at Père Colombe's. She comes in order to rescue him but ends by remaining with him and helping him drink up their money. As she sees the *alambic*, "the shadow of the apparatus, against the background of the rear wall, outlined abominable things, faces with tails, monsters opening their jaws as if to swallow the world." (p. 414) As Zola has shown us earlier in the novel, Gervaise is totally helpless before "the machine to make you drunk," and her paralysis and horror rise to a monstrous hallucination: ". . . she felt herself caught in its copper paws while the liquid flowed in streams through her body." (p. 416) Zola's symbolizing vision explodes in frenzied and demonic phantasmagoria, remote indeed from the allegedly objective and scientific prose of the experimental novel. Yet this visionary projection of reality is not gratuitous or forced; it emerges logically and naturally as an exteriorization and enlargement of Gervaise's felt experience. As she approaches the end of her life, in the midst of her starvation, she stares dumbly at Père Colombe's distillation machine, "sensing that her misfortune came from there." (p. 495) It requires only a brief allusion for the object again to register its symbolic impact.

The role of the documentary in Zola's art must be appraised, not according to his theories, but rather in relation to the essential qualities of his art. In at least some instances in which he relied on a documentary foundation for an episode in his novel, as in the case of Coupeau's delirium tremens, the reader cannot help wondering if the art of the novel is thereby enhanced. Paul Bourget remarked in a letter to Zola: "It is strange, but the delirium tremens, so well described, left me cold," [11] and in *The Gates of Horn* Harry Levin has similarly described the account of Coupeau's death as "narrated with the sententious fervor of a temperance tract." The weakness of this episode might be due to Zola's undue dependence on Magnan's treatise, replete with case histories and scientific evidence, but if documentation threatens to dominate the scene, it does not do so for long. We see Coupeau not only through the detached eyes of the intern at Saint-Anne but also through Gervaise, whose grotesque imitation of Coupeau for the benefit of the residents on the Rue de la Goutte d'Or Zola clearly did not derive from Magnan. When captious reviewers of *L'Assommoir* charged Zola with plagiarism, pointing to seemingly parallel passages in Poulot's *Le Sublime,* Zola admitted his debt at once but at the same time insisted vigorously on the complete freedom of the novelist in the use of his materials. Thus, he declares in a letter to the director of *Le Télégraphe* of March 18, 1877:

> It is quite true that I took some information from *Le Sublime.* But you forget to point out that *Le Sublime* is not an imaginative work—a novel; it is a documentary work in which the author cites oral testimony and true facts. To borrow from it is to borrow from reality.

The distinction between the document and the novel is absolute. Thus, Zola calls special attention to his use of Magnan's *De l'Alcoolisme* but insists that the transformation of the document is his own: "I take my documents wherever I find them, and I think I make them mine." It is precisely within the fictional context that the real gives way to the imaginative: "What is clearly mine," Zola concludes, "are my characters, my scenes, the life of my work—and there you have all of *L'Assommoir.*" There can be no doubt of Zola's keen and passionate awareness of the essential difference between the document and the work of art. The novelist as artist does not copy; he creates.

Zola returned to the question of the scope and limits of documentation in the novel in a letter to *Le Figaro* of June 6, 1896, entitled "Les Droits du Romancier," written in reply to accusations of plagiarism in *Rome* but applicable, as Zola himself contends, to all of his fiction.[12] After citing the principal sources of documentation in his novels—books, oral and written testimony, and personal observation—he states that the aim of documentation is not scientific but novelistic. Bald statements of fact, such as Poulot's *Le Sublime,* express "no imagination, no creative contribution." The art of the novelist resides precisely in his imaginative reordering of experience so as to create an independent universe, like life and yet different from it. With complete justice, Zola insists:

> I am not a scholar, I am not a historian, I am a novelist. . . . my function is to make life, with all of the elements that I had to take wherever they were. . . . Have I given my inspiration to my characters, have I created a world, have I placed beneath the sun beings of flesh and blood, as eternal as man? If so, my job is done, and it matters little where I have found the clay.[13]

Zola's spirited defense of documentation is in fact a noble assertion of the artistic freedom of the novelist, based on the absolute autonomy of the artist in the pursuit of his art. Great novels, Zola implies, can come from any area of human experience, given the requisite poetic power in the hands of the novelist.

From a historical standpoint, the expansion of the language of fiction is one of the foremost accomplishments of the naturalistic novel, and especially of *L'Assommoir*. Zola defends the crudities of his characters as wholly in keeping with their milieu, but his employment of working-class idioms and slang in exposition as well as in dialogue expresses a more fundamental principle of composition: the need for a consistent, harmonious, and uniform style.[14] Here again, Zola postulates the absolute authority of the novelist in the transformation of his material. Not only in direct quotations and dialogue but throughout the novel, Zola employs the idiom of the working class. We can well appreciate the praise of the poet Mallarmé in a letter of February 3, 1877, for Zola's "admirable linguistic attempt, thanks to which so many often inept modes of expression forged by poor devils take on the value of the most beautiful literary forms." In passages of exposition, commentary, and indirect discourse, the language of *L'Assommoir* is that of an observer belonging to the same class and milieu as Gervaise and Coupeau. Marcel Cressot has demonstrated convincingly that, despite Zola's own insistence on the importance of linguistic documentation, the classified lists of popular and slang terms which he compiled by way of preparation were not so much a *lexique* in the strict sense as an *aide-mémoire;* Zola's own knowledge of slang was extensive, and he read Delvau not so much to learn as to be reminded. In fact, a good deal of the slang in *L'Assommoir* is not to be found in any of the dictionaries or manuals with which Zola worked.[15] With all due recognition of his occasional reliance on documentation in his process of composition, his linguistic experimentation in the novel calls our attention to the role of *prématuration,* in Henri Mitterand's useful term, in Zola's art.[16] The documents themselves often serve primarily to stimulate the novelist in the assertion of his originality.

Despite Zola's careful attention to the language of *L'Assommoir* and especially to the demands of "the uniform style," his novel exhibits a variety of stylistic techniques. In his study of stylistic devices in *L'Assommoir,* Jean-Louis Vissière has shown that Zola often employs highly refined syntactical processes, such as the disjunction of subject and verb and of a verb and its object, and the studied dislocation of an adverb for a particular rhythmic or evocative effect. In his bold techniques of stylistic intensification, Zola seems to rival the painters of his day. Yet there are limits to his linguistic experimentation, for he was apparently much more daring in his vocabulary than in his syntax. Even his illiterate drunkards observe the grammatical rules for negatives and for temporal concordance. With all of his deliberate concern for the language of his novel, Zola did not completely succeed in imposing "the uniform style" expressive of the total transference of popular speech to written expression. The aim itself was called into serious question by Flaubert, who distrusted all of Zola's theories. On first reading, he found the novel monotonous, "too long in the same key," but a subsequent reading convinced him of the "real power" of Zola's art.[17] The consistency of style, though only partially achieved, underlies the harmonious and sustained tone of the novel; as Henry James states in his *Notes on Novelists:* "It never shrinks nor flows thin, and nothing for an instant drops, dips or catches." Zola's effort to achieve "the uniform style" is itself a distinct proof of his conscious and radical reshaping of documentation into art.

In a perceptive study of Zola's representation of reality, Gaétan Picon has called our attention to the distinctly poetic character of Zola's language in *L'Assommoir:*

> If he tells us of Gervaise what she herself could not tell us, he does so with the words, the turns of speech, the inflections of Gervaise. And this language which he justifies by a documentary and sociological preoccupation . . . is in reality the coherent expression called forth by an essential transformation of vision.

It is not as a photographer or as a recorder of actuality but as a poet that Zola makes his claim on our attention. For all of its alleged significance in the origin and development of his novels, Zola's documentation is of no terminal value. His documentary sources in *L'Assommoir* are of minor importance alongside of his intuitive grasp and translation of their aesthetic quality. In the novel, the assimilated document becomes an organic part of the fictional context of the work, a context which depends on the fullest possible exploitation of the resources of the art form. No clearer proof of the difference between photography and art in *L'Assommoir* can be found than in Zola's controlled manipulation of point of view, as in the use of Nana to register the impact of Gervaise's sexual fall, Lalie's recognition of Gervaise's alcoholic stupor, and Goujet's view of her abject misery on the streets. Thus, the pathetic death of little Lalie is observed not only by her brutal and drunken father but also by the compassionate and all but sobbing Gervaise. Zola's brief note for the episode in his outline reads simply, *"Un tableau navrant" ("A heart-rending scene")*. In his description of the tortured child's last moments, Zola does not spare the sensibilities of his reader. There is not a shred of the "moral neutrality" or indifference to suffering which some readers have claimed to find in the novel. Zola renders the scene not objectively but with passion and anger, speaking out in his own voice in denouncing "this massacre of childhood" and condemning by implication a society in which the brutalization and murder of children is possible. Perhaps none of Zola's critics has more sensitively responded to his outrage over the moral and physical squalor of French society of the Second Empire than Francesco de Sanctis, who praised Zola warmly for exposing to his countrymen "the misery and the corruption of social classes." The death of little Lalie is itself far more effective than any rhetoric. As Gervaise kneels before the dying child and seeks to give utterance to forgotten prayers, she accentuates the pathos of the scene. Through his skillful displacement of point of view, Zola both mirrors and heightens the events of the novel, expanding the perceptions of his characters into a large and intricate pattern of social relations. In all of these instances, Zola's document serves as a springboard for his imaginative improvisation and art. His preparatory labors must have stimulated his imagination, but they clearly did not displace it.

Zola's *L'Assommoir* offers convincing proof that naturalistic novels at their best are not mere records, but are essentially poetic rather than documentary. It is only recently that the view of Zola as a poet and *visionnaire* has begun to gain ground, yet, as we have seen, Zola himself was keenly aware of the rich imaginative exuberance of his fiction. Despite his scientific pretensions, at least some of his contemporaries—notably Maupassant, Lemaître, Mallarmé, and Verhaeren—saw him as a powerful poet and praised his novels as poems in which reality is transformed and given an independent life. George Moore proclaimed him "the Homer of modern life," and Emile Verhaeren declared that, whatever we may think of Zola's theories, we must view him as a genius of whom all adverse criticism is "vain, useless, besides the point." In our own day, the image of Zola has changed markedly under the impact of the growing conviction that his novels live by dint of their imaginative vitality. Marcel Girard, Guy Robert, Robert Baldick, and Harry Levin are only some of the many interpreters of Zola who refuse to see him as a novelist of historical objectivity and literal exactitude and who direct our attention to his prodigious fantasy. The salient qualities of both lyric and epic poetry enter into his imaginative vision. The language of his novels conforms far less than he believed to the impassivity and objectivity of allegedly impersonal fiction. The massiveness of his art reflects not only the novelist's passion for observation and description but also his love of the excessive and grandiose. As Guy Robert has pointed out, the word "poem" recurs constantly in Zola's outlines and drafts as a descriptive term for his novels; the central function of the document is "in the service of poetic creation." Whatever documentary value the novels may have as representations of history and society, they continue to live not as documents or as statements of doctrine, but as art. As André Gide observes in his *Journal:* "Zola deserves to be placed very high—as an artist and quite apart from any 'tendentiousness' " (entry of October 1, 1934). Zola has been a misunderstood and underestimated writer, in large part because of the limitations of his naturalistic theories. Zola insisted that he was a naturalistic novelist, but it will not do to take him too literally at his word. Zola's naturalism is poetic and not scientific; the theory itself is redefined by the novelist's art.

It would not be difficult to show that Zola was acutely conscious of the exigencies of the novel as an art form. Thus, in a letter of May 24, 1884, to his disciple, Louis Desprez, he criticizes the latter's novel in terms that have nothing to do with naturalism but everything to do with the novelist's command of structure and effect:

> There is no progression of effect, it is a disconcerting hodge-podge which prevents any interest from taking hold. . . . I am definitely for more composed works, where the characters are not crowded against the background because of a lack of perspective. By giving the same value to each episode, you have nothing more than a procession of pages, you do not have a whole.

Zola's consciousness of form and his idea of composition are wholly independent of his naturalism, but they testify to his sensitive grasp as a practicing novelist of the principles and methods of his art.

To appreciate the distinctive values of Zola's art—its large canvas, supple movement, penetrating close-up and mass scenes, and deep compassion and courage—we must read him at his very best, as in *L'Assommoir,* and we must be careful not to confuse his doctrines with his art. Zola's best novels are far greater than his theory of the experimental novel would suggest. His interest in documentation was surely not for its own sake, nor as mere background information, but rather a way of preparing for the act of artistic creation. Documentation may indeed be regarded as Zola's "good conscience" and as a powerful source of assurance in composition. Although there can be no doubt that documentation supplemented and reinforced his great imaginative gifts, the purely documentary values of his fiction are bound to matter less and less as our appreciation of his art continues to grow. As Erich Auerbach has well said, "His image will grow as we gain distance from his time and its problems." [18] In this process of reappraisal, the theories and values of naturalism itself are bound to be modified, no less than Zola modified them in his best work; "a naturalism," as Thomas Mann has tellingly remarked, "that ascends to the symbolic and has close kinship with the mythical." [19]

III
Mann's
Buddenbrooks

Zola's *L'Assommoir* could readily bear the subtitle of Mann's *Buddenbrooks,* "Verfall einer Familie" ("Decline of a Family"), but the resemblance should not be exaggerated. *Buddenbrooks* (1901) conforms only partially and most imperfectly to the canons of naturalism. Nevertheless, particularly in view of the present-day depreciation of naturalistic fiction, it is important to recognize that Mann himself on several occasions referred to his novel as naturalistic. Thus, in the *Betrachtungen eines Unpolitischen,* while pointing to the intensely local and German character of his first novel, Mann also insists that *Buddenbrooks* is a European and cosmopolitan work as well: "It is perhaps Germany's first and only naturalistic novel." [1] Elsewhere in the same essay he refers to *Buddenbrooks* as "a chronicle of city life which developed into a naturalistic novel." We should not infer for a moment that Mann saw himself as a disciple of Zola; he was more familiar with the relatively subdued naturalism of the Goncourts, and he later declared that he had not read any of Zola's work by the time he wrote his first novel.[2] Of course, the young Thomas Mann was well aware of Zola's importance. Moreover, the Norwegian novelist Kielland, who helped inspire Mann in the writing of *Buddenbrooks,* drew directly from the *Rougon-Macquart* in his cycle of novels recounting the decay of a family. The large canvas of *Buddenbrooks* and the pattern of recurring characters drawn from a single family may indirectly reflect Zola's gigantic composition; the naturalism of *Buddenbrooks,* however, depends not on any precise use of French sources, but rather on a common determinism, biological as well as social, that controls the fate of the principal characters. In this respect, *Buddenbrooks* has been described by more than one reader as an "experimental novel." We should recognize, however, that for the young Thomas Mann, and for Zola as well, naturalism is not an absolute, but rather an emphasis, blended with a variety of contrasting styles.

Like Zola's *L'Assommoir,* Mann's *Buddenbrooks* can be viewed in the broad tradition of the social novel, or the *roman de mœurs*. The history of a well-to-do merchant family in a North German port town in the middle years of the nineteenth century, it is at the same time a study of the forces and processes shaping the history of a social class. In presenting both a picture of Hanseatic life and a view of the spiritual history of the European bourgeoisie,[3] the novel in its very conception charges individual experience with broad symbolic implication. Late in life Mann called *Buddenbrooks* "a social novel disguised as a saga of family life," [4] recognizing, however, that no sharp separation can be made between these twin dimensions.

The family experience of the novel is of course that of the family of Mann himself, even though their native city of Lübeck is not identified anywhere in *Buddenbrooks*. The origins of the novel are distinctly autobiographical. Initially, according to the memoirs of the author's younger brother, Viktor Mann, the work was to have been a collaboration between Heinrich and Thomas, in the manner of the Goncourts, with the elder brother writing the family history and Thomas penning its decline. The collaborative plan was soon abandoned, but the conscious parallelism between the Mann family history and that of the family of the novel persisted. Among Mann's literary models, recent Scandinavian novels of business families predominate. In his "Lebensabriss," Mann remarks that initially *Buddenbrooks* was "planned according to the Kielland model of about 250 pages." These were to be divided into fifteen chapters. Once the process of composition was under way, however, the novel seemed to grow of its own accord. As Thomas Mann remarked in a letter of March 27, 1901, to his brother Heinrich, the composition of the novel was animated by a striving for grandeur in form and implication.[5] The resulting length led the publisher to urge that the novel be cut in half and that the descriptive details of social and family history be reduced to make for a more concentrated narrative. The young author insisted, however, that the descriptive and the narrative elements were inseparable, and, after a more than usual delay, the novel was published as he had submitted it. Early critics of *Buddenbrooks* rightly suspected that Mann's main interest lay in Thomas and in Hanno, in the period of decay. The young novelist apparently worked back to his starting point but found in this process that what had been planned as background became part of the foreground, marked by a distinct and independent artistic value.

The history of the composition of *Buddenbrooks* has been considerably illuminated in recent years, notably through the studies of Dr. Paul Scherrer and also through the publication of a substantial part of the written documentation for the novel. Both the planning and the redaction seem to have been careful and leisurely, extending over more than three years, from June 1897 to August 1900. During this period, and particularly in the early months, Mann took great care in ordering both the total design and the individual details of his huge canvas. The broad panorama was suggested, at least in part, by literary models, English and Russian as well as Scandinavian and French. Paul Scherrer has called our attention to Mann's notebook notation of 1897: "Grünlich's bankruptcy. See *Mahlstroom*." [6] The reference is to a short novel of the Norwegian writer Jonas Lie, which recounts the financial ruin of a well-to-do and respectable business family. Antonia Grüner, wife of the ruined financier, presents at least some similarity to Tony Grünlich in Mann's novel. A more compelling literary model must have been Tolstoy's *War and Peace,* not only in the areas of resemblance between the Bolkonsky and Buddenbrook households but also in the thematic and philosophical preoccupations of the two novels. Alois Hofman has called attention to the similar reflection of large social relationships in the crises of individual characters in the novels of Tolstoy and Mann. The representation of death in *Buddenbrooks*—indeed, the lingering obsession with death and the intimate hovering over the most minute details of physical dissolution—would also seem to suggest a kinship to Tolstoy's great novel. It is no surprise, then, to learn from Viktor Mann that the young author had a picture of Tolstoy before him on his desk during the writing of *Buddenbrooks*. As Mann later declared, Tolstoy's moral energy and gigantic epic power helped to sustain him as his youthful novel grew larger and larger.

However large and pervasive the inspiration of other novels may have been, there can be no doubt that Mann's documentation depended principally on his own experience and his recollections of family life in Lübeck, and on the conversation and written accounts of older members of the family. A variety of materials was available to him. In a letter of May 11, 1937, Mann states that in the writing of *Buddenbrooks,* "I worked with the help of family papers and information concerning business activities which I brought from my native city." [7] The family journal which mirrors the crucial events in the lives of the Buddenbrooks is similar to a journal which was handed down from one generation to another in the Mann family.[8] In his passion for exactitude in documentation, the young novelist seems to have explored every avenue of information at his disposal. The testimony of his brother Viktor is revealing:

> The young author had received from his mother all the old family papers, faded notebooks, letters, party souvenirs, and records of the family tree, which were to be found in trunks and drawers. He asked many questions about this and that episode, and also read excerpts of his manuscript to the family.

We may assume that at these family readings additional details of relevant family history were elicited. In addition to oral testimony from members of the family near at hand, Mann solicited detailed accounts from other relatives, notably from his sister Julia, his Aunt Elisabeth, and his father's cousin Consul Wilhelm Marty, who sent long typed pages full of information. A substantial report by Julia of considerable importance and excerpts of a letter from Aunt Elisabeth constitute invaluable material for our study, for they enable us to catch at least a glimpse of the young Thomas Mann in his workshop;[9] however, a great deal of other source material, including the details supplied by Wilhelm Marty, has not yet come to light. Paul Scherrer has published a list of questions sent by Mann to Consul Marty and a reproduction of one page of the reply.[10] These materials and Thomas Mann's notebooks for the planning of *Buddenbrooks* are in the collection of the Thomas Mann Archives in Zurich; it is hoped that they will soon be published in their entirety. In any event, although we are not likely ever to know what information Mann may have garnered from family conversation, the large role of the author's personal experience in the making of *Buddenbrooks* is attested to by his later assertion, "the whole novel takes its life from memories of youth," and serves again to remind us of the impossibility of our ever knowing all of the primary sources of documentation for this or for any novel. The description of houses, streets, places, and scenes need not have come from any external source, nor was Mann obliged to use external aids in order to reproduce the dialect of either Lübeck or Munich.[11] Nevertheless, a notebook entry under the heading "Permaneder" includes a detailed list of Munich idioms and slang, which may have been compiled with the help of a dictionary. Mann's efforts to supplement his personal experience were assiduous. Even so marginal a detail as a traditional family recipe for carp cooked in red wine was the subject of interrogation of his mother, Julia.[12] We can assume that other recipes and similar details of family lore were taken directly from the old family journal.

In addition to his use of documentation for the broad outline of family history and for countless incidental details of everyday life in the nineteenth century, Mann drew on family records and recollections, written as well as oral, for much of the characterization in the novel. The recently published documents of the Mann family suggest that the model for the Consul, Johann Siegismund Mann, was just as fond of genealogy and of circumstantial detail as his novelist grandson. It would be incorrect and unjust to insist on an absolute correspondence between the members of the Mann family and the principal figures of *Buddenbrooks;* yet events in the lives of members of the Mann family enter directly into the shaping of their counterparts in the novel. Many, if not all, of the main characters were modeled on individuals whom Thomas Mann either knew personally or who were known to older relatives still alive at the time the novel was written. Naturally, in depicting a character somewhat remote from the immediate present, such as the elder Johann Buddenbrook, Mann had to rely considerably on old portraits or photographs and on general historical and background information. In the case of the three children of the Consul, it is clear that Thomas, Christian, and Tony possess at least some of the traits and undergo some of the misfortunes of the novelist's father, Senator Thomas Mann, the senator's brother, Onkel Friedel, and Tante Elisabeth. We may see a clear parallel to Thomas Buddenbrook in Mann's remark in his "Lebensabriss" that his father was a highly respected and influential citizen, "but for years no longer took much pleasure in the course of his business affairs." Viktor Mann's account of a visit to Onkel Friedel offers at least partial confirmation of a degree of similarity with Christian in the novel. In the instance of Elisabeth, we may see an elaborate and sustained parallel, in both individual characteristics and in the salient events of private life, to her counterpart, Tony. Viktor Mann reports that after the publication of *Buddenbrooks,* Elisabeth's friends began calling her Tony, a practice which at first made her indignant but which later she accepted with good humor and pride. Nevertheless, we must recognize that in all of these instances of similarity between the fictional character and the model in real life, there are important differences which attest to Mann's readiness to alter and reshape actuality freely, according to the artistic needs of his novel.

Precisely because of Mann's bold imaginative approach to his materials, his novel will not support a literal and thoroughgoing identification of the members of his family with their fictional analogues. There are innumerable discrepancies in chronology, ranging from approximately five to twenty years, because the author places the events of the novel further back in time.[13] Thus, Thomas Buddenbrook is born in 1826 and dies in 1875, whereas Senator Thomas Mann was born in 1840 and died in 1891. In apparently only one instance does an event in the novel occur later than its historical counterpart: the death of the "à la mode-Kavalier," Lebrecht Kröger, father-in-law of the Consul. His death, vividly narrated, is a direct consequence of his seething hatred for the *canaille* during the revolution of 1848, but his model, Johann Heinrich Marty, actually died in 1844, and it was the model for the father of the Consul, the elder Johann Siegismund Mann, who died in 1848 as a result of a heart attack brought on by the uprising. In the novel, the old man dies seven years earlier. The transposition of roles is not fortuitous; Lebrecht Kröger with his perfect correctness and aristocratic bearing may well be expected to react to the revolution with intense fury; yet his sense of dignity and propriety obliges him to suppress his anger. His heart attack and death follow naturally, not only from his temperament but also from his inner demoralization and frenzy all during the events of the day. A more striking and more significant departure from reality is the fate of Hanno. The death wish that animates Hanno is the surest proof of the exhaustion of the Buddenbrook family, but the title of Viktor Mann's memoirs, *Wir waren Fünf* (*We Were Five*), is eloquent testimony to the large gap separating life and art. Even in a spiritual or symbolic sense, it would seem wide of the mark to argue for more than a partial identification between Hanno and his creator, even though they share a common position in the sequence of generations. According to his subsequent remarks, Mann seems to have felt closest to Thomas, but he clearly cannot be identified with any of his characters.

Despite its many divergences from historical reality, when *Buddenbrooks* appeared, its characters seemed close enough to recognizable models for residents of Lübeck to consider it a *roman à clef*,[14] and it seems to have aroused considerable indignation in the author's native city. Perhaps the most painful aspect of the young novelist's reliance on actuality has to do with the use of Onkel Friedel as the model for the unfortunate Christian

Buddenbrook. Viktor Mann assures us that his uncle lived in Hamburg in an apartment, not a mental institution, and died in 1926 in perfectly sound mind; he does not tell us, however, how deeply his uncle was wounded by the representation of his counterpart in the novel. On October 28, 1913, Friedrich Mann inserted the following notice in the *Lübeckische Anzeiger:*

ADVERTISEMENT

In the course of the past 12 years, through the publication of

Buddenbrooks

written by my nephew, Herr Thomas Mann of Munich, I have incurred much that is unpleasant and that has had most painful consequences for me, among which is the current publication of Alberts' book, *Thomas Mann und seine Pflicht.*

I therefore find myself impelled to turn to the *reading public of Lübeck* and to ask that the aforementioned book be evaluated appropriately.

When the author of *Buddenbrooks* drags his closest relatives in the dirt by means of caricature and makes a public mockery of their life history, every right thinking man will find that this is reprehensible.

It is a sad bird that fouls its own nest!

Friedrich Mann, Hamburg.[15]

We do not know if Friedrich Mann's nephew replied to his uncle in any way. It is evident that Onkel Friedel had harbored his feelings for several years before giving vent to them in public. His complaint is directed not so much at Wilhelm Alberts as at the novelist, for all that Alberts states in his book, *Thomas Mann und sein Beruf* (*Thomas Mann and His Vocation*),— Friedrich Mann's mistake in the title is not wholly besides the point—is that Thomas Mann used close relatives as models for some of his characters. Alberts singles out no one, and Friedrich Mann may have been unduly sensitive. Nevertheless, the episode reveals that the novelist's dependence on reality is plainly not without its perils for both the writer and his models. Onkel

Friedel is surely neither the first nor the last model to protest against his fictional representation. It may well be that in the portrayal of Christian the distance between the fictive and the real is far less than for most of the other characters in the novel. The danger of inflicting suffering is inherent in the method. In his essay, "Thomas Mann und die Wirklichkeit" ("Thomas Mann and Reality"), Paul Scherrer shows that even Mann's love letters to his future wife are used in his fiction. In his important essay of 1906, "Bilse und Ich" ("Bilse and I"), Mann states: "The reality which a poet makes use of for his own purposes may be his daily life, may be the persons who are nearest and dearest to him." He goes on to add that the new artistic reality is essentially different from actuality, but Friedrich Mann's complaint is a moving reminder that this is not always the case.

Unquestionably, many of the peculiarities and mannerisms of Mann's characters are transposed directly from life and are an important element of the sense of authenticity in the novel. Nevertheless, the dislocation of reality is far more significant than its literal transference. Despite external similarities, Christian is not Onkel Friedel any more than Tony is Tante Elisabeth or Hanno is Thomas Mann; the characters in the novel live and breathe in their own right in the pages of the book. As Ernst Bertram contends, Mann may portray his characters from models, "but his portraits are new men." His family history was an indispensable starting point for the young novelist, but to the extent that his characters and events take on autonomous life and movement, he has succeeded in appropriating reality and making it his own.

Like Zola following the publication of *L'Assommoir,* Mann was charged with plagiarism in *Buddenbrooks,* notably in the course of a lawsuit in 1906. A certain Lieutenant Oswald Bilse had written a novel of army life, *Aus einer kleinen Garnison,* and was sued in court in Lübeck for having slandered his regiment. Mann's novel was cited along with Bilse's as evidence of the common tendency of novelists to draw directly on life and to represent living persons in their work. We should note in passing that Theodore Dreiser wrote a foreword to an American edition of *Life in a Garrison Town* in 1914 in which he acclaimed Bilse's novel as "sound realism, and . . . because of it, good art." For Dreiser, Bilse's novel was justified by its boldness and honesty of subject matter, reflecting its author's keen sense of observation; Bilse's colportage was essential, Dreiser claimed, to the truthful delineation of life.

For Thomas Mann, Bilse's novel pointed to a dangerous confusion of the fictive and the real. Mann was not exactly flattered by the linking of *Buddenbrooks* and Bilse's novel and felt impelled to respond to the larger question of the relation of a work of art to actuality in his essay, "Bilse und Ich." Above all, Mann says, the novelist is essentially a poet; as such, he depends not on *Erfindung* ("inventing") but on *Beseelung* ("inspiriting"). The presence or absence of a model in the process of composition is of no importance whatsoever; the writer, through the poetical transformation of his material, "makes the substance of the work a part of himself." Thus, Mann insists on "a fundamental difference" between the reality drawn upon in the making of a work of art and the work itself. In response to the offended reactions of some citizens of Lübeck to his novel, he asks:

> What has the real Lübeck of today to do with the work which took me three years to construct? Stupidity. . . . When I have made a sentence out of something, what has that something to do with the sentence? Philistinism . . .[16]

Art, according to Mann's spirited defense, is perforce a subjective deepening of reality; the making of an art work is an act of free creation, independent of the claims of any physical model. In a letter to Kurt Martens on March 28, 1906, Mann reiterates his position:

> I should like to refer to the error that a reality with its artistic representation lies therein, which can be identified in a practical way. I should like to think of the work of art as an absolute. . . .[17]

In defense of his art, Mann cites the example of Goethe and Tolstoy and of other great novelists of the past: "I say that very great poets have invented nothing in the course of their lives, but have only filled their souls with what they have inherited, and given it new form." It is precisely this power of inspiriting and shaping anew that is the hallmark of the great artist. It is worth pointing out that Tolstoy himself was confronted with exactly the same problem by those readers of *War and Peace* who saw the novel as mere colportage. In reply to a relative who wrote asking him to identify the prototype of Prince Andrei, Tolstoy insisted:

> Andrei Bolkonsky is nobody—the same as any character by a novelist as opposed to a writer of memoirs or personalities. I would be ashamed to appear in print if all my work consisted of copying portraits, making enquiries and memorising.[18]

In a similar vein, Thomas Mann could argue that Thomas Buddenbrook is nobody in that he derives his value from what his creator has made of him, whether the material facts of his existence have their counterpart in real life or not.

Twenty years after the polemics of "Bilse und Ich," Mann returned to the problem of the relationship of art to reality. In an essay of major importance for the understanding of his work, "Lübeck als geistige Lebensform" ("Lübeck as a Spiritual Form of Life"), Mann declares that art "is something symbolic. It is the new realization, on another plane, of an inherited form of existence." Art is thus both a repetition and a transformation of reality, at once like life and essentially different from it. Again, applied to *Buddenbrooks,* the rights of the novelist are absolute. It is noteworthy that his brother novelist, Heinrich Mann, who also contributed material for the novel, supports Thomas Mann's position completely:

> That which is essential, its coherence, the direction in which all the characters moved, the idea itself, belonged only to the author.

The interplay of the fictive and the real in *Buddenbrooks* merits detailed examination. Owing to the recent publication of some of Mann's source materials, we are able to see in specific passages exactly what Mann borrowed and how he transformed his sources. On September 8, 1897, Thomas Mann's sister Julia replied to a letter from her brother requesting details of the private life of their Aunt Elisabeth and of her daughter Alice. The reply, a document of several pages, is intimate and frank, and we can well appreciate Julia's plea in a covering letter that her essay be used with discretion, especially since many of the principals, including the counterpart of Grünlich, Ernst Elfeldt, were still alive.[19] The knowledgeable reader of Julia's account will find echo after echo of phrases and situations in the novel, dealing not only with the experiences of Tony but with her parents and grandparents and their milieu as well. Nevertheless, the occasional parallel passage serves primarily to point up the difference between the factual description of Julia's essay and the fictional context of expression in the novel.

Julia's memoir offers a rather full account of Aunt Elisabeth's two marriages and describes in some detail the circumstances leading to her first marriage in May 1857. The first visit of Elfeldt occurred precisely as does Grünlich's visit in the novel, unexpectedly, while the family was sitting in the garden, although late in the evening rather than in the afternoon. Julia describes both the charming effect Elfeldt had on Elisabeth's parents and the unconcealed aversion in which he was held by Elisabeth. Soon afterward, Elfeldt met her on the street after failing to find her at home. Julia reports the following brisk exchange:

> "Alas, young lady, how sorry I was not to be able to meet you at home, and how delighted I am to see you now." "The pleasure is not mutual," she said rudely, and walked on past him.

This brief exchange of two sentences is expanded by Mann into three paragraphs, without any previous transition, at the very beginning of Chapter II of the third part of the novel:

> "How sincerely grieved I was, young lady, to have missed you," Herr Grünlich said several days later, when Tony, who

was returning from a walk, met him at the corner of Breiten-strasse and Mengstrasse. "I took the privilege of paying my respects to your mother, and it pained me deeply that you were not at home. How delighted I am nevertheless to meet you now."

Fräulein Buddenbrook had stopped when Herr Grünlich began to speak, but her eyes, which she had half closed and which suddenly became dark, did not look higher than Herr Grünlich's chest, and about her mouth played the ridiculing and utterly merciless smile with which a young lady sizes up and spurns a man . . . Her lips moved—what should she answer? Ha! It would have to be a word which would reject and destroy this Bendix Grünlich once and for all, but it would have to be a clever, witty, crushing word that would at once pointedly wound and impress him . . .

"The pleasure is not mutual," she said, keeping her eyes fixed on Herr Grünlich's chest; and after she had shot this carefully poisoned arrow, she let him stand there, threw back her head, and—red with pride in her sarcastic readiness of speech—went home where she learned that Herr Grünlich had been invited to a veal roast the next Sunday. . . . (I, 125–126)

The substance of the exchange is precisely as it is reported in Julia's essay, but the context is the ironic interplay of the unc-tuous and calculating Grünlich and the proud and self-conscious Tony. It is the voice of the narrator that provides the ironic tone, but the style is fully in keeping with the event; only a mo-ment after Tony believes that she has shattered Grünlich with her *schlagendes Wort* ("crushing word"), she learns that her parents have invited him to dinner on Sunday. The narrator's account, in *style indirect libre,* of Tony's bold and sarcastic re-solve, is openly comic in the markedly disproportionate relation-ship between ends and means. The scene oscillates rapidly be-tween extremes: Grünlich's elaborate politeness and Tony's mocking scorn; but it is Grünlich who emerges triumphant from the occasion, for the final revelation of his impending return on Sunday retrospectively colors all that has gone before. We learn from this encounter, as well as from other episodes, that Tony is not really clever at all but simply has an exaggerated opinion of her self-assurance and intelligence, and we see too that Grünlich is more than a match for both her and her well-meaning parents. Julia's memoir furnished the novelist with the raw material for the scene, but its elaboration within the context of the novel belongs to Mann alone. The reference in Mann's notebook in which he planned the sequence of the novel is nothing more than the briefest notation: "Weiteres Auftreten Grünlichs" ("Further Appearances of Grünlich");[20] we must assume that Julia's report was close at hand during the process of composition. Nonetheless, the contrast between the source and its fictional transformation is impressive. The interiorization of action, subtle characterization, trenchant irony, and enlargement of the episode within its larger social context are all the work of the novelist. The document is essential as a starting point, but it is only that and nothing more. Tony and Grünlich in the novel take on a richer, fuller, and qualitatively different existence from Elisabeth and Elfeldt, although the real historical circumstances which served as a point of departure are still present, in transmuted form, within the novel.

Similar examples of individual passages could be multiplied readily. More important, however, are the large divergences in the novel from the historical events recounted in Julia's essay. In the midst of Elfeldt's importunate suit, Elisabeth went on a vacation to Stettin to stay with good friends, the Bartels family, and while there, she was courted by young Heinrich Bartels, whose feelings she shared. This episode is transformed into the idyllic visit to Travemünde and the brief romance with Morten Schwarzkopf, but with the significant difference that young Bartels was a member of one of the wealthiest and most prominent families in Stettin, whereas Morten is a poor student. Paul Scherrer has suggested that the paucity of details concerning Elisabeth and Heinrich Bartels in Julia's memoir may have been to the novelist's advantage. Clearly, the role of class and social status in the value system of Tony and her family is brought out far more sharply in the novel than in the anecdote, but, in addition, the adventure itself of Tony and Morten is tender and poignant, and it stays with Tony all during the remainder of her hard existence. Still another interesting area of difference between the novel and historical actuality is Elisabeth's second marriage, with one Gustav Haag, part-owner of a hardware factory, who seems to have possessed all of Permaneder's grossness without any of his amiability. Tony's judgment of Permaneder is clearly not that of Mann himself; Permaneder's easy informality and hearty good will are a breath of fresh air amid the cold correctness of the Lübeck merchant aristocrats. A principal source for the delineation of Permaneder may well have been a caricature published in *Simplicissimus* in 1897. Still other major divergences from actuality in the novel have to do with the history of Elisabeth between the time of Elfeldt's bankruptcy and her return to the family home, a period of dire poverty in which she lived with her destitute husband in a small town in the Lüneburger Heide. Mann spared Tony this suffering, for in the novel she returns to her parents' home as soon as Grünlich's ruin is made evident. From these and many other similar examples, we can see that, in the composing of *Buddenbrooks,* Thomas Mann drew freely and imaginatively on the details in the lives of his models, collapsing and fusing some details, ignoring others, inventing still others, and translating fact to the plane of independent fictional reality.

No doubt other documents will in time come to light that will illuminate the relationship of Mann's novel to its historical sources. It is reasonable to suppose that such purely historical events as the Napoleonic occupation of Lübeck and the "lübische Revolution" of 1848 were drawn in part from standard historical studies. Other sources are neither historical nor biographical but philosophical—in the writings of Schopenhauer and Nietzsche—or musical—in Mann's employment of what he called "the epical motif technique" popularized by Wagner. André von Gronicka has suggested that Mann's use of the leitmotif may owe less to Wagner than to Tolstoy and to Dmitri Merezhkovski's analysis of Tolstoy's art. The description of Hanno's rapturous musical improvisation is a parody in words of Wagnerian music, but, as Ronald Peacock has shown, the principle of the leitmotif pervades the entire novel in the subtle interweaving of key images and symbols. In the descriptions of places and things as well as in the exploration of inner life, Mann moves from exactitude of detail to a rich pattern of symbolic figurations. Jean Royer has sensitively analyzed the metaphorical function of the Gothic buildings and the quaint street scenes of Lübeck, which are presented in the novel both scenically and panoramically, as from the opposite ends of a telescope. We should note that Mann, in *Betrachtungen eines Unpolitischen,* spoke of the fullness and massiveness of the novel as "Gothic, not Renaissance." The association of characters with particular places and the repetitions and variations in physical description transform objects into symbolic expressions of inner feelings. The orchestration of philosophical themes and ideas has the same function and reflects a similar assimilation of source materials. Mann's use of complex artistic and ideological analogies contributes markedly to removing the novel from the limited plane of a family chronicle; for the young novelist, the background of ideas is ultimately just as real and as vital as the background of events. There is, however, this central difference: although the historical events support and extend the naturalistic values of the novel, the ideological elements all contribute to a subjectifying of experience and a consequent mitigation of naturalism that becomes more and more evident as the novel moves toward its conclusion.

Buddenbrooks thus asserts the somewhat paradoxical condition of a naturalistic narrative presented in a variety of techniques and styles that have very little relation to strict naturalistic representation. There can be no question of the operative force of the social code of the milieu. It is proper for Tony to obey her parents and marry Grünlich, but in retrospect we acquire a true appreciation of their well-meant advice and the values on which it rests. The biological determinism is even more thoroughgoing. Despite Thomas' correctness and his determination, "die *dehors* zu wahren" ("to preserve appearances"), his true physical condition belies his outward pose. He shares the bad teeth of his family and dies after a visit to the dentist. The physical debility and social waywardness of Christian are explained even by his father in genetic terms, when he blames the easygoing bent of Lebrecht Kröger for the dissoluteness of his son:

> He will be happy that his frivolous blood and his impious inclinations will continue to live, not only in Justus, the playboy, but also visibly in one of his grandsons. . . . (I, 104)

The fate of Justus Kröger's sons, Jürgen and especially Jakob, is at least an indirect illumination of the destiny of their cousins and of the Buddenbrook household. Little Hanno is intuitively conscious of his role as the last *Stammhalter* and the incarnation of the Buddenbrooks' destiny: "they must give up on me; I came out of a decayed family." (II, 457)

For some readers, this decay is emblematic of the decay of the entire social order depicted in the novel, and it has even been argued that the fate of Thomas and Hanno is a representation of the fate of the German nation in the twentieth century. The Buddenbrooks clearly do not typify Germany, and one may rightly ask with Jürgen Kuczynski if they are even representative of the North German merchant class to which they belong. Mann is implicitly critical as well as admiring of the Buddenbrooks, but his view of their class is impersonal and objective. The decline of the family is a mode of social displacement but not a reflection of a generalized process; the social function of the Buddenbrooks will be performed by others. Heredity and its physiological consequences play a far more coercive role in the novel than environment, and both are defined within the strict context of the decay of the Buddenbrook family.

In true naturalistic fashion, the account of Hanno's death reads like a case history of typhoid fever. Here the scientific documentation becomes obtrusive through the refusal of the novelist to particularize Hanno's experience. The language is cold and abstract, and the reader must make the necessary application to Hanno's fate; yet, even here, Mann does not explain the course of the disease solely in physiological terms but in accordance also with the patient's will. Hanno dies, presumably, not simply from typhoid fever but from "fear and rejection of the voice of life." In any event, Hanno must die for the sake of the narrative, even though Mann dispatches him with undue coldness and celerity and pays for this rigorous naturalistic consistency with a loss in artistic effectiveness. Perhaps the distancing of Hanno's suffering and death was a consequence of the long series of preceding deaths. Nevertheless, despite the intensity of Mann's concentration on the details of the cessation of life, his deaths are not nearly as harsh or as violent as we generally find deaths to be in other naturalistic fiction. We should recall the declaration of Zola's most avowedly naturalistic American follower, Frank Norris, that "terrible things" must happen to the characters of the naturalistic novel. Norris' canons may describe quite well the naturalism of Zola or of Norris himself, but they apply only partially to the more muted and more introspective naturalism of Thomas Mann. It is true that in the dentist's chair Thomas Buddenbrook undergoes brutal torture, and Mann's description of his suffering is indeed terrifying. The reader is himself with Thomas, indeed inside Thomas, in the dentist's chair, his suffering rising to "an inhuman pain that tears his whole brain apart" as the extraction fails and the crown of the tooth breaks off. Thomas' harsh and sudden death is a direct result of this excruciating assault on his whole being. The episode is climactic, but it is not at all typical of events in the novel. For the most part, life in the Buddenbrook family flows evenly and undramatically, with no more violence than an occasional quarrel between Thomas and Christian. For although their passions and tempers mount to the point of verbal violence, the tension is soon dissipated in reflection and confession. As Thomas justifies his own one-sided and inadequate mode of life to Christian, he admits: "I have become what I am because I did not want to become like you." (II, 247) From the available documentary sources, we have no knowledge of whether Senator Thomas Mann and Onkel Friedel ever quarreled as do their counterparts in the novel, nor would it be of the slightest importance if they had. Both Thomas and Christian act in accordance with their characters; despite their radical opposition in temperament, they share a common destiny shaped by the relentless pressure of biological law.

From the very beginning of critical response to *Buddenbrooks,* many of its readers called attention to its naturalistic values. Samuel Lublinski, whose review of the novel Mann especially admired, spoke of the author's "strict naturalistic objectivity" and described *Buddenbrooks,* as Mann himself was later to do, as the "first and only naturalistic novel," akin to naturalistic drama in its directness and specificity. Ernst Bertram emphasized the objective portrayal of scene and character in the novel and saw Mann's method of ironical distancing as similar to the processes of clinical anatomy. Alexander Pache claimed that *Buddenbrooks* is "one of the most important novels that we owe to the naturalistic movement," and that "Mann wields all the weapons of naturalism with cutting inexorable sharpness." Arthur Eloesser called it an "experimental novel in a much more definite sense than that of Zola." In our own day, Eberhard Lämmert reminds us in a penetrating essay of the fundamentally naturalistic character of Mann's novel. Yet, this approach is by no means a common one at the present time, partly because of the generally held assumption that naturalism and art are incompatible and also because the tendentiousness characteristic of German naturalistic drama is almost wholly absent in Mann's novel. Only in the account of Hanno's typical school day do we find an element of direct social criticism. As a consequence of German unification, the school has become "a state within the state," wherein each student is subjected to Prussian discipline and uniformity. Mann's assault on the educational system, as Richard Hamann and Jost Hermand have shown, is markedly akin to that of Holz and Schlaf, Hauptmann, Heinrich Mann, and other German writers in the naturalistic tradition. Yet it must be recognized that Hanno's difficulties at school also reflect his essential difference from his classmates and his awareness of his alienation as an artist. Even this single example of overt social criticism is mitigated in its context. Mann's muted note of protest is in sharp contrast to the strident denunciations of social evil characteristic of most naturalistic fiction. It must also be noted that his novel is incomparably richer than most other naturalistic novels in the subtlety and complexity of its art.

We should fail to take adequate account of the force and implications of *Buddenbrooks* were we either to ignore the presence of large naturalistic elements in the novel or to view Mann's naturalism as divorced from his art. Nowhere is Mann's artistry more apparent than in his skillful employment of parallels and contrasts,[21] in such instances as the fate of the Ratenkamp family, former proprietors of the house on the Mengstrasse, whose ruin is explained deterministically by the Consul during the dinner at the housewarming in the beginning of the novel; in the parallel relationship of Tony and Morten and of Tom and little Anna; and in the bitter coincidence of the celebration of the anniversary of the firm and the financial catastrophe which follows Thomas' repudiation of the watchword of his ancestors. Parallelism not only contributes to the abundance and variety of the action but also provides both prospective and retrospective illumination of the history of both individuals and the family as a whole. The implicit commentary of the parallel is frequently reinforced by the voice of the narrator, a voice that is often ironic but also warm and humorous, providing both intimacy and knowledge, and thereby drawing the reader closely into the world of the novelist's creation. The narrative voice, as Wolfgang Kayser has shown, is itself a fictive creation into which the author has transformed himself. In *Buddenbrooks,* the fictive narrator maintains a resolutely ironic distance from his characters and events.

Nowhere, perhaps, is Mann's irony more intricate and ambiguous, or more remote from rigorous naturalistic premises, than in the representation of the final stage of the history of the Buddenbrooks. If biologically the fate of Hanno seals the decay of the family, it also marks the culmination of a long process of refinement and growth. Many of Mann's critics, such as Ernst Bertram, Arthur Eloesser, Hellmuth Petriconi, and Eberhard Lämmert, have recognized the ironic dimension of the *dénoue-*

ment. It is to the credit of the young Rainer Maria Rilke that, in a review of the novel in 1902, he grasped most perceptively the ambiguity of the notion of decay as expressed in Hanno:

> To him once again the possibility of an ascent is given (to be sure, a different ascent from that which the Buddenbrooks hope for): the infinitely perilous possibility of a great artistic life, which will not be fulfilled.[22]

Thus, Thomas Buddenbrook's dark references to "the retrogression . . . the descent . . . the beginning of the end" (II, 55) must all be reappraised in the light of the positive gain in the quality of human experience represented by Hanno. Beyond the fate of Hanno, however, is a darker ambiguity and irony, in the final lines of the novel, wherein the pathos and suffering of existence is evoked by Tony's lament—"Alas, it is so hard and sad" —unrelieved even by the defiant faith of Sesemi Weichbrodt. We can understand why Kurt Martens could describe *Buddenbrooks* as "annihilating," but Mann's rejoinder, insisting on the positive and affirmative values of the novel, is more in keeping with its spirit and total effect: "Yet every good book which is written against life is a temptation to life." [23]

Thomas Mann's dependence on documentation in the composition of *Buddenbrooks* must be viewed not simply as an expression of naturalistic poetics but also as a first step in the artist's structuring of experience. As in our discussion of Zola, we may conclude with assurance that Mann's careful investigation of historical reality and his reliance on solid empirical foundations provided him with a sense of sureness and confidence in the composition of his novel. It is remarkable, all the same, how little emphasis the recently published portions of the outline and notebooks seem to place on documentation, despite Mann's elaborate system of cross references and his scrupulous classification of notes for characterization under the heading of "Anecdotes, Character Traits, Peculiarities of Speech, etc." [24] It would appear that, even in his notebooks and plans for the novel, Mann sought to eliminate any sign of dependence on literal sources and to enlarge the distance separating fiction from reality. In the very conception of the novel, however, this separation could not be maintained in pure form. We should not criticize Mann for his pillaging of family archives. His documentation provided him with suggestions in both large and small details which he was able to re-create artistically. Without these suggestions, *Buddenbrooks* might well have been a different and a poorer novel.

Like Zola and indeed like all great novelists, the author of *Buddenbrooks* demands to be read first and foremost as a poet. Once again, the response of the poet Rilke confirms the claims of Mann himself. In his sensitive review of *Buddenbrooks,* Rilke admits that, to write his novel, Mann had to become a chronicler, but the chronicle is transformed into rich imaginative expression through Mann's capacity "to be a poet, and to fill many figures with convincing life, with warmth and substance." Although Mann considered his novel as personal and provincial, "indeed regionally and locally defined," it is the surest proof of the shaping power of art that *Buddenbrooks* draws its readers into its world, making them part of its author's "Hanseatic homeland," and it a part of them, wherever their dwelling place may be.

IV
Dreiser's *An American Tragedy*

The development of naturalism in the United States in the closing years of the past century reflects the impact not only of Zola and his followers but also of powerful currents of thought and expression in England and America that impelled writers toward a more accurate representation of reality than conventional moral canons permitted. Many of the young novelists who shared the new passion for candor and exactitude in art had served their apprenticeship as newspapermen and wrote of life as they saw it with the eyes of reporters, concerned above all with the clear and straightforward delineation of facts. For Dreiser, as for many of his contemporaries, this newspaper experience was of considerably greater importance than the emulation of literary models, even though models were not lacking. In 1893 the city editor of his St. Louis newspaper advised the young Dreiser to read Balzac and Zola; he followed half of this advice, moving avidly from one novel of Balzac's to another. In a letter that appears to have been written on May 14, 1916, he assures H. L. Mencken, "I have never read a line of Zola." Even so, Dreiser was well aware of Zola's program, and he responded warmly to the emergent naturalism of the day.

Dreiser's view of human experience was developed without any direct dependence on Zola's naturalistic doctrines, but, even as a young man, he subscribed unreservedly to the naturalists' objective and clinical view of human behavior and to the rigorous determinism which Zola and his followers saw as governing human events. Dreiser's reading in 1894 of popularizations of philosophy and science by Herbert Spencer and Thomas Huxley was of decisive importance; later, he remarked to Frank Harris that Spencer "took every shred of belief away from me; showed me that I was a chemical atom in a whirl of unknown forces." [1] He also read Charles Darwin and applied Darwin's principles of the struggle for existence and the survival of the fittest to the situation of the individual in American society. In an article published in February 1897 in *Ev'ry Month,* a magazine Dreiser edited for a music publisher, he states flatly: "It is only the unfit who fail," and in an article published in the *Chicago Journal* on March 18, 1914, he says of Chicago: "It is a big city where men must fight and think for themselves, where the weak must go down and the strong remain." In similar vein that same year, in an interview published in the *New York Evening World* for June 18, he remarks apropos of his novel *The Titan* in the classic language of social Darwinism: "Nature is unscrupulous! She takes her way, regardless of the suffering caused, and the fittest survive."

Dreiser's social Darwinism was accompanied by a thoroughly mechanistic view of human behavior. In the years immediately prior to the writing of *An American Tragedy,* he was fascinated by the writings of the scientist Jacques Loeb, whose books, such as *The Mechanistic Conception of Life* and *The Physiology of the Brain,* he read enthusiastically. He found confirmation for his deterministic convictions in Loeb's insistence that ethics and indeed all human principles and actions are based on instinct and are at bottom chemical in origin. Dreiser would have vigorously endorsed Taine's celebrated maxim that virtue and vice are products, like sugar and vitriol. Life for Dreiser was a jungle in which only brute force triumphed. On December 18, 1924, in the midst of the composition of *An American Tragedy,* he wrote Upton Sinclair, "I see the individual large or small—weak or strong as predatory and nothing less." [2] Clearly, Dreiser's harsh and uncompromising view of human behavior is in complete accord with naturalistic doctrine. The individual is the helpless prey of biological and social forces and must dominate them or else succumb. The role of the novelist is to dramatize the operation of these forces as they are in life: the struggle for existence depicted in his novels is presumably that of everyday existence in modern America.

Even before writing *An American Tragedy,* Dreiser was described by V. L. Parrington as the chief of American naturalists. It is not likely that Dreiser would have found the phrase inappropriate or objectionable. His critical formulations are often reminiscent of Zola's. Thus, in his foreword to the 1914 edition of Bilse's *Life in a Garrison Town,* Dreiser declares:

> What we need, and what the social intelligence of the world rejoices in, are true, unflinching pictures or presentations of life done after and through a temperament which is artistically sound.

Dreiser's assertion of the novelist's task reechoes Zola's famous formula: "Une œuvre est un coin de la nature vu à travers un tempérament" ("A work of art is a corner of nature seen through a temperament"). In a letter of October 10, 1915, to H. L. Mencken concerning films which he hoped to help produce, Dreiser remarks: "I can't begin by ramming naturalism down their throats—not at least until I get my hand in. . . ."[3] Yet, in his novels Dreiser had been ramming naturalism down the throats of the reading public for several years. All of his early novels—*Sister Carrie* (1900), *Jennie Gerhardt* (1911), *The Financier* (1912), *The Titan* (1914), and *The "Genius"* (1915)—are squarely within the naturalistic tradition, not only in their pervasive determinism but also in their dependence on literal reality. The point of departure for *Sister Carrie* is the elopement of Dreiser's sister Emma in 1886 with one L. A. Hopkins, a cashier who stole from his employers' safe. The story of *Jennie Gerhardt* is based on the experiences of two of Dreiser's sisters. Frank Cowperwood, the hero of *The Financier,* is drawn after the tycoon Charles T. Yerkes, and *The "Genius"* is patterned largely on the life of Dreiser himself. In addition to employing particular models for his characters and events, Dreiser based all his books on careful and extensive research. In the course of his long career, he accumulated immense files of materials for his work. Not only did he seem to save everything but his memory and power of recall seem to have been extraordinary. All of Dreiser's fiction is marked by his passion for exactitude as well as by his preoccupation both with individuals and with the large natural and social forces that direct and determine their fate.

An American Tragedy (1925) is probably Dreiser's best novel. It is the only one which was a popular success, and its reception did more than any other single event to establish him in the front rank of modern American novelists. Huge in conception and massive in bulk, it constitutes the summation of Dreiser's career as a novelist, bringing the distinctive qualities of his art to their fullest realization.

Despite the fact that his formal education was limited and he was not well-read in the great literature of the past, Dreiser approached his art with as much dedication and seriousness of purpose as any of the great European masters. The composition of *An American Tragedy* required five years, from 1920 until November 1925, but he had meditated on the subject of the novel for several years before beginning work on it. In a letter of April 20, 1927, commenting on the origins of his story of crime and punishment, he remarks:

> I had long brooded upon the story . . . so common to every boy reared in the smaller towns of America. It seemed so truly a story of what life does to the individual—and how impotent the individual is against such forces. My purpose was not to moralize—God forbid—but to give, if possible, a background and a psychology of reality which would somehow explain, if not condone, how such murders happen. . . .

We can see how powerfully his naturalistic values entered into Dreiser's formulation of his aims. The enormous effort he made to ground his novel solidly in material reality offers an example of fidelity to lived experience that outrivals even that of Zola or Thomas Mann.

As is well known, the death of Roberta Alden and the subsequent trial and execution of Clyde Griffiths in *An American Tragedy* are based on a celebrated murder case of 1906 in Herkimer County, New York: the trial and conviction of Chester Gillette for the murder of Grace Brown. Gillette, a supervisor in his uncle's factory in Cortland, New York, had seduced one of the working girls, Grace (or "Billy") Brown, who became pregnant and demanded that he marry her; Gillette had the prospect, however, of marrying into a wealthy and socially prominent family in his uncle's circle. On the pretext of marriage, he persuaded Grace Brown to accompany him to Big Moose Lake in the Adirondack Mountains; there, while they were boating, he struck her on the head with a tennis racket and drowned her. The trial received a great deal of coverage in the newspapers across the country, and Dreiser, who was working as a magazine editor at the time, read newspaper accounts of the proceedings and clipped them for future use. We know, however, that he considered a large number of similar cases before finally selecting that of Chester Gillette. Over several years, Dreiser had compiled a notebook, entitled *American Tragedies,* containing notes on fifteen cases, all of which presented instances of murder motivated by social ambition.[4] He was particularly attracted to a case of 1911 in which a Baptist minister, Clarence Richeson, murdered a poor country girl whom he had made pregnant and who stood in the way of a wealthy marriage. Dreiser actually wrote six chapters of a novel based on the Richeson case before abandoning it for the story of Chester Gillette. It has been suggested that he selected the Gillette case because of the easy availability of documentation, but he also chose it because he considered it richer in its social and psychological problems. In a journalistic report on a similar case, written in 1935, he remarked that, from the time of his days as a newspaper reporter in 1892, he had observed the repeated occurrence of a type of crime wherein a young, ambitious youth trapped between two girls, one rich and the other poor, attempts to escape from his entrapment through murder.[5] Dreiser considered the Gillette case as completely representative, both in its details and in its causes; Gillette was driven not by "murder for murder's sake" but by "those dreadful economic, social, moral and conventional pressures about him." No doubt Dreiser felt that these pressures were more palpable and also potentially more dramatic in the Gillette case than in the other similar cases that he studied. The details of the Gillette case were for him most nearly typical of a kind of murder which he considered to be virtually an annual occurrence in America, at least since the 1890s.

Just as the selection of his particular model was the result of careful deliberation and study, so in the process of documentation itself Dreiser was highly selective as well as elaborate and thorough. His documentary efforts were fitted closely into the emerging pattern of his novel. Uppermost in his mind in planning the novel was the story of the hero's crime and his subsequent trial and punishment. It is therefore no surprise to find Dreiser's documentation concerned exclusively with the second and third books of the novel, and particularly with the court proceedings and their aftermath. The account of the discovery of the murder in the novel embodies several details from the news report printed in the *New York Daily Tribune* for July 14, 1906, including the false identity of the murderer, the finding of the hat, and the chance encounter of the fleeing culprit in the woods.[6] Dreiser gave special attention to the details of Chester Gillette's trial, most notably the opening speeches of the attorneys, the testimony of witnesses, the legal strategies of both sides, and the summations of argument. The judge's charge to the jury was apparently lifted verbatim from the *New York World* for December 5, 1907,[7] and many other similar examples could readily be pointed out. The love letters of Grace Brown to Gillette had been reprinted in the leading New York newspapers, and Dreiser borrowed several passages from them, not without occasional amplifications, for the letters of Roberta Alden to Clyde Griffiths. It has been estimated by Emil Greenberg that, in all, Dreiser derived about thirty pages of his novel directly from the accounts of the trial and from the letters. The presence of these documents in the novel, even in modified form, is characteristic of Dreiser's mode of composition, but when we recall that the novel is 840 pages long, the borrowings take on considerably less significance. Our primary concern is not with the mere identification of Dreiser's documentary sources, but with their integration into the novel as a whole. There can be no doubt that Dreiser's frequent modification of the language of his sources was made in view of the specific demands of his characters and situations. Nevertheless, textual parallels are unmistakably present in the novel, and it does not aid in the understanding of Dreiser's art to deny their existence any more than it does to exaggerate their importance.

The composition of *An American Tragedy* seems to have proceeded smoothly, if intermittently, until June of 1923, when Dreiser felt the need to visit the scenes of the events in the Gillette case. That summer he traveled across a large section of the relevant area of upstate New York, concentrating on Cortland, where the Gillette factory was located, and on Big Moose Lake. He covered the various neighborhoods of Cortland carefully, noting the physical peculiarities of the poor sections of the town and of the residential areas of the well-to-do. From Cortland, he drove to South Otselic, where Grace Brown had lived. Helen Dreiser has observed that the narrow country road leading to Grace Brown's home was "about the same as Dreiser described it in the book." More important, the feeling of the emptiness and drabness of Roberta Alden's life was suggested directly by the shabbiness and isolation of the lonely farmhouse, which was perched on a hill under large trees. Dreiser also drove to Herkimer, the county seat, where Gillette's trial was held, and to the lake country, and to the scene of the murder there. He stayed at the same lodge as had Gillette and Grace Brown. The boat attendant at the lake boathouse, who turned out to be the same attendant who had served the luckless couple seventeen years earlier, described details of the event to Dreiser and pointed out the spot on the lake where the murder occurred. Dreiser rowed to this very point on the lake; the vividness of atmosphere and landscape in the account of Roberta's drowning reflects the acuteness and sensititivity of his powers of observation.

It was in all likelihood immediately after this visit that Dreiser completed Book II of the novel, which culminates in

Roberta's death and Clyde's flight. As soon as he had finished his tour of the area, he rented a cabin in the woods and spent the remainder of the summer working on the novel. Recent observations evidently played an important part in Dreiser's literal rendering of details. It should be noted, however, that he apparently did not attempt to seek out any of the individuals who had participated in the Gillette case, although he probably could have done so with little difficulty. His documentation was directed to places and things far more than to individuals.

Although the journey in the summer of 1923 constituted Dreiser's most extensive documentary exploration, he followed it with other similar travels, such as a trip to a shirt factory in Troy, New York, to observe the manufacturing of men's collars and the physical arrangements inside the factory. For the writing of the final scene in the novel, he visited Sing Sing prison. Afterward, dissatisfied with his presentation of prison life in the novel, he made a second visit, in November 1925, while the proof sheets of the novel were waiting to be corrected. On this occasion, armed with credentials designating him a newspaper reporter for the *New York World,* he was able to visit and study the death house and to talk to a criminal awaiting execution.[8] In all likelihood, Dreiser's visitations were accompanied by rapid note-taking, either on the spot or shortly thereafter.

In addition to visiting scenes of events of the novel, Dreiser sought the advice of experts on specific problems. Relatively early in his labors he consulted the Freudian psychiatrist A. A. Brill on the psychology of murder, and as he proceeded into the legal intricacies of Clyde's trial, he enlisted the aid of his lawyer, Arthur Carter Hume, in whose building Dreiser rented an office. There he wrote the concluding chapters of the novel. Located in the same office building was a lawyer and ex-banker, J. G. Robin, who also advised on the details of the novel following Clyde's arrest and imprisonment. No doubt, still other experts were consulted orally for specific needs. In addition to its thoroughness, Dreiser's documentation seems to have been rigorous in its economy and wholly professional in its manner. In every instance of his preparation, we can see an experienced reporter at work. He seems to have had a keen eye for the usable detail, as well as a rare sense of efficiency, for he usually needed but a single brief visit to acquire a grasp of the distinctive character of a place or event. The feeling of authenticity pervading *An American Tragedy* owes everything to Dreiser's passion for documentation as the cornerstone of his art.

We can readily see the many similarities, both broad and detailed, between the real experience of Chester Gillette and Grace Brown and their fictional counterparts. The physical circumstances of the murder seem to be almost the same, and Clyde's subsequent history tallies very closely indeed with Gillette's. Innumerable details could be cited in addition to those mentioned above. For example, it was Gillette's attorney who insisted that the accused was no murderer but "a mental as well as a moral coward," as is claimed in Clyde's defense by his lawyer. According to the newspaper reports of the trial, Gillette declared before the passing of sentence: "I am innocent of the crime as charged in the indictment and therefore I think it should not be passed." In the novel, Clyde protests his sentencing in practically the very words of Gillette: "I am innocent of the crime as charged in the indictment. I never killed Roberta Alden and therefore I think this sentence should not be passed." (p. 809)[9] More important still for our understanding of Dreiser's naturalism in the novel is the insistent pressure of the milieu. The force exerted by the environment on the characters and events is a direct expression of the novelist's knowledge and experience of the physical setting. Clyde and Roberta are delineated in intimate association with their environment and, indeed, could not be conceived apart from it. Their individual fate is inseparable from the pressures of their society.

It is precisely when we examine these pressures that Dreiser's modifications of the historical reality underlying *An American Tragedy* take on full significance, for he did not hesitate to depart from his documentary sources whenever the larger conception of his novel demanded it.[10] Thus, in the novel Clyde's poverty is stressed from the very first pages. Never for a moment are we allowed to lose sight of the meanness of his daily life and his gnawing desire to escape somehow from the privations of the poor. Chester Gillette, however, came from a middle-class background that was quite unlike the milieu of Clyde's youth. For Dreiser, Clyde's poverty is so bitter and his desire to escape from it so intense as to justify even murder. By dint of his poverty, Clyde stands forth more clearly than Chester Gillette as a critique of the ethic of material success at any price. Yet this ethic is but a logical expression of the struggle for existence and the survival of the fittest. Clyde's values are thus wholly in keeping with the accepted norms of his society as Dreiser views and describes them.

It is from the vivid memory of his own poverty as a boy and from the sordid details of his own childhood and adolescence that Dreiser derived much of the material for Book I of the novel. When Dreiser was eight, his sister Mame, then sixteen, became pregnant by a local attorney in Terre Haute, Indiana, and a country doctor refused to perform an abortion. The child, stillborn, was buried secretly at night. Another sister, Sylvia, was later made pregnant by the son of a wealthy family. When he refused to marry her, she was sent off to an older sister in New York to have her baby there. The fate of Clyde's sister, Esta, in the novel, closely parallels that of Dreiser's own sisters. In other respects too, Clyde is closer to Dreiser than to Gillette. The novelist's father, for example, was as fanatical in his piety and as blind to the practical affairs of life as is Clyde's father, who supports his family marginally at best through mission work and an occasional odd job. Helen Dreiser has called our attention to a similar combination of economic misery and religious fanaticism in the landlord's family in the Los Angeles apartment building where she and the novelist lived in 1919 and the desperate longing of the young daughter to escape from the meanness of her milieu. The absolute contrast in the novel between the worlds of the very poor and the very rich and the desperation of Clyde's desire to escape from poverty finally force him to contemplate Roberta's murder.

Nevertheless, Dreiser makes it clear beyond any doubt that, although Clyde plots the murder, he stops short of physically carrying it out. Whereas Gillette deliberately struck Grace Brown on the head with a tennis racket, Clyde accidentally strikes Roberta with a camera; moreover, Gillette apparently drowned his victim, but Clyde, by doing nothing, simply allows Roberta to drown. She is actually submerged by the wale of the boat striking her on the head. Clyde longs for her death and plans it; yet, he leaves the scene with the thought that "after all, he had not really killed her." (p. 532) It is reasonable to suppose that Dreiser was influenced here by the defense strategy in the Gillette case, but, although in the events of 1906 the accident is at best only a possibility, Dreiser presents it in his novel as a fact. We know, therefore, that Clyde causes Roberta's death when he does not wholly mean to do so, and this knowledge places his conviction and execution in an ambiguous light. In a letter of March 10, 1931, Dreiser describes Roberta's drowning as "the planned culmination of a series of inescapable circumstances"; it is nonetheless an act for which Clyde cannot be held altogether to blame. As in *Sister Carrie,* the role of accident contributes to a mitigation of personal responsibility and guilt. Quite apart from his account of Clyde's trial, Dreiser suggests by his essential modification of his source that his hero is a victim of injustice at the hands of society.

The question of Clyde's guilt aroused considerable discussion among lawyers, and one of the most prominent criminal attorneys of the day, Clarence Darrow, assured the novelist that it was impossible to determine Clyde's guilt with certainty on the basis of the novel. For Dreiser, however, even Chester Gillette was innocent. His crime was the result, not of an act of will, but of overpowering external forces:

> Not Chester Gillette . . . planned this crime, but circumstances over which he had no control—circumstances and laws and rules and conventions which to his immature and more or less futile mind were so terrible, so oppressive, that they were destructive to his reasoning powers.[11]

This defense applies with even more cogency to Clyde Griffiths, who is clearly the victim of forces he does not understand and from which he cannot escape. His values are perforce those of American society, and it is precisely because of his representative significance that Dreiser called the novel *An American Tragedy*. F. O. Matthiessen has pointed out that the original title for the novel was *Mirage*. Clearly, Clyde has the wrong values and substitutes them for the reality under his feet. The wealth and status to which he aspires vanish just as they are within his reach. Dreiser's publisher, Horace Liveright, urged him not to entitle his novel *An American Tragedy,* but Dreiser refused to change it, insisting on the typical character of his hero and the causal dependence of his fate on his society. The novelist was also asked by his publisher to change the name of his hero to "Ewing or Warner or some other good representative name" on the grounds that Griffiths was too difficult to pronounce.[12] Here again, Dreiser refused, doubtless because he considered it vital that the hero of his novel have the same initials as Chester Gillette. In his arresting and challenging title, Dreiser implies forcefully that not Clyde but American society is responsible both for Roberta's fateful accident and for Clyde's subsequent punishment.

Dreiser's indictment of the American social order cuts deeply into the fabric of its judicial institutions. The jury system itself as employed in criminal proceedings is viewed by the novelist as wholly incapable of rendering justice. We know that Clyde does not willfully cause Roberta's death; yet he is convicted of murder in the first degree. In a letter of April 25, 1931, Dreiser remarked that the judgment of Clyde in the novel is "by an ignorant, conventional and revengeful background of rural souls" who "judge him far more harshly than would individuals of deeper insight and better mental fortune." Dreiser so presents Clyde's trial and conviction as to convey the appearance of a fair trial; the outcome of the proceedings, however, appeals to the reader's sense of injustice, heightening his indignation and his feeling of sympathy for the helpless victim.

Dreiser's alterations of his sources in both the social background and circumstances of his hero and in the details of the crime are so far-reaching in their consequences for our understanding of the novel that his incidental changes of names and places are of relatively little import. Such changes in place names as from Cortland to Lycurgus, South Otselic to Biltz, Big Moose Lake to Big Bittern Lake, and Herkimer to Bridgeburg provide only the thinnest layer of fiction over the solid foundation of fact on which the novel rests. Similarly, Dreiser altered the name of the judge from Devendorf to Oberwaltzer and that of the governor from Hughes to Waltham. For knowledgeable readers, Dreiser's novel must have appeared as a *roman à clef* at the time of its publication.

More significant by far are Dreiser's modifications of details for the sake of a larger artistic purpose. Thus, in the Gillette case, the boat was not used as an exhibit during the trial, whereas in the novel the boat is brought into the courtroom for the reenactment of Roberta's drowning. As a result, Clyde is compelled to relive the moments of the catastrophe and to undergo even more acutely his earlier shock and pain. The boat is not of any essential importance in the trial, but its psychological function as a direct source of Clyde's suffering is crucial. It becomes an integral part of the two-track narrative of the courtroom sequence, whereby Clyde is simultaneously the object of legal prosecution and the participant in the painful events of the past. The stark interaction of past and present overwhelms him and reduces him almost to the condition of a dumb animal unable to escape from his torture and thereby rendered pitiable as well as helpless. The boat serves as only one part of this psychological process, but it is an important part and Dreiser dramatizes it effectively. The fictive re-creation of events at once embodies and transforms the underlying reality.

Even the comparatively few instances of the verbatim reproduction of documentary materials in the novel must be appraised in their artistic context. Immediately following Clyde's final plea to the court—"I think this sentence should not be passed"—Dreiser shifts the perspective from Clyde to his mother seated nearby:

> And then staring straight before him conscious only of the
> look of admiration and love turned on him by his mother.

For had not her son now declared himself, here at this fatal moment, before all these people? And his word here, if not in that jail, would be true, would it not? Then her son was not guilty. He was not. He was not. (p. 809)

The mother's love and simple faith in her son's goodness lend pathos and tenderness to the harsh event, as Clyde's assertion of innocence is reflected through his mother's passionate conviction. Clyde's terse statement, taken almost literally from the transcript of the trial of Chester Gillette, is given a distinct contextual value, illuminating the character and feelings of his mother and anticipating her role in the conclusion of the novel. Just as Clyde Griffiths is not Chester Gillette, so Clyde's mother is not the mother of Gillette, even though the texts of their telegrams to the governor on the eve of the execution are virtually identical. One of the most moving and most vivid episodes in the novel is the interview between Mrs. Griffiths and Governor Waltham. So overcome is Clyde's mother by her suffering that she cannot utter more than a few sentences, but they are enough to articulate the depths of her "agony in this hour." The serious and conscientious governor, who bases his decision on legal grounds alone, represents the absolute antithesis of his petitioner, whose speech is moved not by reason but by simple piety and uncontrollable feeling. The contrast is emphasized by the inability of Reverend McMillan, as Clyde's spiritual adviser, to offer any support to Mrs. Griffiths' assertion of her son's innocence, and so both the governor and the minister serve as unconscious instruments of the cruelty and injustice of society. No documentary material in and of itself could have enabled Dreiser to dramatize the suffering of the mother and invest her with dignity and grandeur of spirit. The historical reality provides a point of departure and a direction for the scene, but its intensity and evocative power are the creation of an artist and not of a mere recorder of actuality. Here, as throughout the novel, the poignant and arresting portrayal of character in moments of crisis forcefully asserts the dominance of the fictive over the real in Dreiser's art.

For all of his reliance on literal sources, Dreiser was

acutely aware of the artistic demands of his novel. In a letter of July 16, 1924, to his wife, Helen, written in the midst of his work on *An American Tragedy,* he complains of the difficulties of composition:

> It seems simple. I know the story. The right procession & selection of incidents should be as nothing but it just chances to be everything. And so I write & rewrite.[13]

The proper selection and arrangement of incidents preoccupied Dreiser incessantly both within his chapters and in their interrelations. Many passages were rewritten four, five, and six times. One chapter was completely rewritten seven or eight times and then dropped. Over a million words long, the original manuscript was fully three times the length of the 840 pages finally published. All during the course of composition and especially as the novel neared completion, it underwent drastic cutting by Dreiser's typist-editors and by Dreiser himself. He deleted nine additional chapters describing the milieu of Clyde's impoverished childhood. Chapter VIII in this sequence, published in *Esquire* in 1958, offers a penetrating illumination of Clyde's early consciousness of his poverty and his abject position in society. It thereby reinforces the elements of social and psychological causation. The quality of insight into character in the deleted chapter suggests that other rejected chapters may also have been worth saving. Dreiser's cuts seem to have been motivated mainly by his concern for the form of his novel: the reduction of the early history of Clyde places in bolder relief his adventures in Lycurgus and the subsequent catastrophe.

By dividing his novel into three principal parts, Dreiser sought to impose a structure of causal relations, with the first part presenting Clyde's childhood and youth; the second, his experiences in Lycurgus, culminating in Roberta's drowning; and the third, the trial and punishment. Unquestionably, Dreiser could have encompassed Clyde's fate in considerably less than 840 pages; yet the massiveness of detail and the concentration on crucial scenes is essential to the novel's effectiveness. Book I is a prelude, illuminating Clyde's character in all its weaknesses and establishing the social and psychological roots of his subsequent misfortune. Book II, despite its length, is marked by a strong sense of the dramatic rising out of Dreiser's sensitive portrayal of intimate character relations and their culmination in violence. It is Book III which is the most questionable from a structural standpoint. The presentation of the trial extends over 100,000 words, replete with details that are often merely circumstantial. As F. O. Matthiessen observes, here "the novel becomes documentary in the most literal sense." Nevertheless, as we have seen, even in the trial sequence Dreiser makes the most significant details part of the larger fictional context. Even if he was unduly influenced by the fullness of his documentation in the depiction of Clyde's trial, here, too, the novel is more than a rambling and diffuse transcript of court proceedings. Although it seems clear that Dreiser's documentation is far better integrated into the novel in Book II than in Book III, nowhere during the course of the trial is the use of documents random or capricious. The trial itself, as Régis Michaud points out, imposes a pattern of orderly presentation, beginning with the selection of the jury and the opening pleas, and proceeding to the examination of witnesses, their cross-examination, the examination of the defendant, the calling of further witnesses, the final pleas, the charge to the jury, the deliberation in the jury room, the verdict, the final statement of the defendant, and the pronouncement of sentence. The relentlessness and inevitability of the sequence of events in the courtroom are an analogue on a smaller scale of the coercive movement of the novel as a whole.

Dreiser's novel exhibits a consciousness of form and a skill in selection and arrangement that many of his critics have been reluctant to acknowledge.[14] There is considerable evidence within the novel of Dreiser's careful attention to its organization. The precise attention to the time scheme, particularly in Book II, but in the other sections as well, not only provides precision and verisimilitude but, by forcing our attention on the step-by-step progression of events, also fixes them within a time-bound perspective. The inexorable flow of time within the fixed limits of the action down to the day and the very hour of Clyde's death in the electric chair encloses and defines the novel's deterministic universe. A similar structural device is Dreiser's employment of parallelism, most notably in the conclusions of the first and second books. As Book I closes, we see Clyde fleeing from Kansas City to escape complicity in a fatal automobile accident after a joy ride in a borrowed car. Dreiser describes him crawling like an animal toward the south, with his hands and knees in the snow, hoping to hide, "to lose himself and so escape—if the fates were only kind—the misery and the punishment and the unending dissatisfaction and disappointment." (p. 161) But the fates are not kind. Dreiser's portrayal of Clyde's demoralized flight is an ironic foreshadowing of his later flight through the dark wood to the south after the drowning of Roberta.

Perhaps the most recurrent technique Dreiser employs to order the events of his novel is his use of large social institutions to fix and define the social situation of his hero. The mission operated by Clyde's parents, the Green-Davidson Hotel, the Lycurgus society, the collar factory, the summer resort, the courtroom, the death house—all of these are organizing centers of action that illuminate Clyde's behavior in shifting perspectives.[15] Dreiser not only enlarges Clyde's perception of society; he makes us see the force of the milieu in shaping his development. The bustling commotion of the big hotel, with its mixed opulence and tawdriness, arouses the acquisitive and sensual desires of the young bellboy, thereby contributing at least indirectly to his disorientation and ruin. Yet the hotel is a mirror of the turbulence of American life itself, its raw vitality and vulgarity as well as its ambition and promise. Just as the factory represents hierarchies of power and the great houses on Wykeagy Avenue are embodiments of authority and wealth, so all of Dreiser's institutional settings are at once physical and symbolic landscapes, simultaneously things and analogues of social forces that surround and define characters and events. The symbolic projections of milieu become part of the education of the reader even more than of Clyde Griffiths. It would seem difficult, in the case of Clyde, to speak of a significant "quest pattern" in Dreiser's novel, for Clyde lacks sufficient insight into his condition to be aware of any pattern in his acts. Through the careful juxtaposition of scene and event, Dreiser exposes to the reader not only the backwardness and simple-mindedness of his hero but also the complexity of the institutions that lure and finally overwhelm him.

Irony is yet another structural principle in the novel. We have already indicated the darkly ironic culmination of Book I in relation to the climax of Book II. An equally striking example is the frame enclosing the novel. The first chapter presents the bedraggled group of gospel singers with their Bibles, hymn books, and tracts carrying on their missionary work on the street corner of a large city. At the end of the novel, in an epilogue entitled "Souvenir," Dreiser returns to that scene. Clyde's parents are older now, and the mother's face is "broader and more characterful than her husband's, but more definitely seamed with lines of misery and suffering." A small, absent-looking boy is also present, the Griffiths' grandson, Esta's child. The resemblance to Clyde's initial situation and circumstances is unmistakable. The frame points clearly to the recurrent pattern of the collision of the individual and society, not necessarily in the Griffiths family, but in Clyde's inevitable successors in the social order. The epilogue is thus a return to the beginnings of the novel and also a commentary on the individual fate of Clyde as part of a fixed and cyclical pattern of American experience.

The ironic perspective of the novel is reinforced by countless particular instances. Clyde begins at the "Door of Hope" mission, and he ends in the electric chair. His meeting with his uncle in Chicago opens the door to eventual power and wealth, but in Lycurgus the "lucky break" turns to dust and ashes. In the death house, a fellow criminal who befriends Clyde leaves him two books, *Robinson Crusoe* and *The Arabian Nights,* both expressive of a world of romantic fantasy to which he aspires but will never know. The execution itself is ironic, for we know that Clyde did not murder Roberta, even though he planned to do so. As Richard Lehan points out, the irony in the novel, in both its large and incidental expressions, constitutes a bitter commentary on the fate of Dreiser's hero. From the first page to the last, he is marked as a victim of circumstances he is power-less to combat. He is sacrificed not simply to a malign social order but to a pitiless, implacable destiny that places even his loftiest dreams and hopes in a brutally ironic perspective.

If the attacks on the structure of Dreiser's novel have been unjust or of only partial and very limited validity, this is clearly not the case as far as his hero is concerned. Clyde Griffiths is so weak and imperceptive that he cannot carry even the representa-tive and typical function which Dreiser assigns to him. Although Clyde's fate is both the story of an individual and a case history, the fundamental mediocrity of the hero weakens both his partic-ular and his symbolic role. Early in the novel Dreiser provides several examples of Clyde's weakness and helplessness, as in his financial relations with his mother and in the use made of him by Hortense. Clyde is not simply unlucky; he is stupid, an easy dupe, less than typical in both intelligence and acquired knowl-edge. Passive and bewildered in the face of complex human problems, when he is caught between the conflicting claims of Sondra and Roberta, he is demoralized and torn apart. Perhaps Clyde's passivity is necessary as a demonstration of the iron law of determinism, but the gain in rigor is at the expense of interest and even, at times, of credibility. In Book III, at the trial, Clyde is so hopelessly confused that he does not seem to realize what is happening to him, and he goes to his death without understand-ing for a moment what his life was all about. Clearly, what mat-ters for Dreiser is not so much Clyde himself, but his fate as a projection of social forces.

If Dreiser's naturalism is far more effective in the represen-tation of milieu than in the depiction of character, it is nonethe-less modified and redefined in accordance with the novelist's temperament. The cruelty of fate is attenuated, not by any act of heroic virtue on Clyde's part, but by the deep and pervasive compassion of Dreiser himself for the pain and suffering of his victims. The voice of the narrator is an insistent presence that colors the action and mediates between the reader and the plane of events. We need only recall the tenderness of the portrayal of the first meeting of Clyde and Roberta and the rapture of their first kiss and the joys of young love that follow. Perhaps Dreiser describes this love so tenderly out of the realization that it represents Clyde's happiest moments, for they do not last. According to his editorial assistant, Sally Kusell, as Dreiser wrote the scene of Roberta's drowning, he wept copiously.[16] We can imagine a similar involvement on the part of the novelist in the moving interview of Clyde's mother and the governor. It was no doubt this same compassion that decided Dreiser not to present the execution of Clyde, but rather to indicate its effect through the anguish of Reverend McMillan and Clyde's mother. This art of dramatic suppression is at sharp variance with naturalistic representation; neither Zola nor any of his more recent followers would have turned away from a culminating act of terrifying violence, nor does Dreiser himself altogether turn away from it. We feel the death of Clyde and we know that it has occurred, even though we do not see it. Dreiser's refusal to sensationalize or even to describe Clyde's death enables him to intensify the pity which dominates all other feelings in the novel.

Dreiser's compassion is not mere sentimental emotionalism, but an implicit qualification of the uncompromising social Darwinism to which he seemed, in theory, to subscribe. No reader of *An American Tragedy* can doubt that Dreiser cares deeply about the victims of social processes. At the same time, his condemnation of the jungle of American society is a refusal to accept the brutalization of the weak and the helpless in the name of the survival of the fittest and points toward the need for a new, more humane order of social values and relations. As the novel moves to its conclusion, Dreiser's pity for his victim often turns to anger and takes the form of blunt social preaching. His portrayal of death row is not only vivid writing; it is also a searing condemnation of "all that could possibly be imagined in the way of unnecessary and really unauthorized cruelty or stupid and destructive torture." (p. 815) If at this point the novelist seems to yield to the moralist, we should not forget that Dreiser's angry assault on institutional abuses is in the great tradition of the social novel of the nineteenth century as we find it in Balzac, Dickens, and Tolstoy. We may sense a similar anger in Dreiser's novel at the use of religion as fraud or evasion. The final appeal of Clyde's mother to a religious sanction of value is an empty and pathetic gesture. Yet, there is a measure of genuine consolation for the pain of her bereavement in the depth of her love for her son. More profound than even his bitter protest of injustice, Dreiser's pity for human suffering enlarges his novel to cosmic dimensions.

We do wrong to both Dreiser and ourselves to see him, following the usual cliché, as a great writer who wrote badly. It is perfectly true, as Lionel Trilling remarks, that "few critics have ever been wholly blind to Dreiser's great faults"; nevertheless, the faults have diminished in importance as the appreciation of the power of Dreiser's art has grown. Certainly, it is much more possible to appraise Dreiser as a serious artist today than was the case a generation ago. This is not to deny that he has faults, but to place them in a wider perspective. Dreiser's style is wholly adequate for his purposes in *An American Tragedy*. Abstracted from the flow and cumulative force of his novel, there is no doubt that his language is often wordy, repetitious, and clumsy. His idiom is essentially that of the late nineteenth century and is as dated as his social philosophy. The remarkable achievement of *An American Tragedy* lies in the power of the novel to triumph over its very real weaknesses. We may grant that the structure of the novel is imperfect, that Clyde is drab and colorless, that the style is defective, and that the ideological premises are simplistic; despite these strictures, however, the novel sustains an intensity of passion and poignancy that is rare in the annals of fiction.

Novelists, like other writers, create as they can and as they must. Dreiser was more dependent on literal reality than perhaps any major naturalistic novelist of his time. Much of his best writing depends heavily on his deliberate study and observation. His great strengths reflect his sensitive awareness of both the scope and the limits of documentation in fictional creation. Plainly, he knew the difference between the literal transcription of a documentary source and its transformation into art. At the time of its publication, hostile critics of *An American Tragedy* contended that Dreiser had stolen his novel from court records and newspaper reports. Helen Dreiser has reported the novelist's indignant response to these charges. Dreiser's defense, strikingly reminiscent of the spirited replies of Zola and Mann to similar charges, is a bold assertion of the absolute freedom of the artist in the pursuit of his art:

> No one creates tragedies—life does that. Writers report them, and after all, Goethe copied his Faust from Dr. Faustus and so, by the critic's standard, should have been charged with stealing the old legend of which, throughout Europe, there were a dozen versions. And what about Shakespeare? He should have been charged with stealing *Antony and Cleopatra, Julius Caesar* and *The Merchant of Venice,* in fact, every play he ever wrote, barring none.[17]

For Dreiser, "copying" is inherent in creation. All writers "steal" in that they derive their material from life, and even the freest works of invention are based on the experiences and art of others. Yet the truly gifted artist makes what he borrows his own. As Dreiser insisted to Dorothy Dudley, *An American Tragedy* was "*his,* quite his." The history of Chester Gillette was but a point of departure, wholly different in quality and significance from the created experience of Clyde Griffiths. To the extent that Dreiser's novel lives, his characters and events, like the novel itself, have their own independent value.

There are, to be sure, instances in which the fusion of the fictive and the real in Dreiser's novel is imperfect. At times, as in the courtroom sequence, the pressure of actuality becomes oppressive, and the plane of human relations is overwhelmed by inert objects and facts. Nevertheless, the undeniable pressure of documentation is almost always controlled by Dreiser's primary concern with the human drama in the interaction of his characters. Despite incidental lapses, he dominates his documentary material at virtually every point in the novel, reshaping the literal groundwork of events through the power of his art. Made vivid and endowed with new life, Dreiser's documents no longer remain the same.

Documentation was both a necessity and a source of

strength for Dreiser. Yet, despite the great importance he attached to literal reality in the writing of all of his novels, it would be easy and inaccurate to exaggerate this importance and to view Dreiser not as a novelist, but as a journalist and historian who uses the novel as a pretext. Dreiser's *An American Tragedy,* like all great novels, carries its own justification. In its sureness, intensity, and massive power, Dreiser demonstrates as conclusively as do his European counterparts that naturalism and art are not incompatible.

At its best, Dreiser's fiction is a modified naturalism, strikingly akin to the naturalism of Zola himself in the inconsistency of its theory and practice. Eliseo Vivas rightly emphasizes the wide distance separating Dreiser the mechanist and Dreiser the novelist in concluding that "Dreiser is a better artist than his philosophy permitted him to be." Even though *An American Tragedy* embodies Dreiser's deterministic convictions, the novel triumphs over his determinism. Although naturalistic values are markedly present in the novel, they operate far less rigorously in their artistic context than they do in Dreiser's general formulations of doctrine. His determinism is far more of an emphasis than an absolute. His naturalism, like that of Zola and indeed of all significant naturalistic novelists, is personal and subjective. Francesco Binni has called attention to the cult of energy and the mystical affirmation of the totality of life in Dreiser's novels. Especially in his later years, Dreiser was more aware of the limitations of scientific law than of its demonstrable operation in human affairs. All of his novels, early and late, go well beyond his mechanistic ideological assumptions and the alleged historical and social objectivity of his art in their expression of an intense and powerful personal vision.

Only recently have readers begun to appreciate Dreiser as an artist. When Dreiser's art first began to be considered seriously in America, V. L. Parrington wrote of his "vast and terrifying imagination." In the sweep and energy of his vision and in his symbolizing power, Dreiser, like Zola, raises naturalism to the level of high art. And again like Zola, it is essentially as a poet that Dreiser makes his largest claims on our attention.

On the appearance of *An American Tragedy,* Joseph Wood Krutch hailed it as "the greatest American novel of our generation." For a new generation, it is well on the way to a position of classic importance among the landmarks of the American novel. Robert Penn Warren has recently described the relentless logic of the novel as "the poetry of destiny." Indeed, Dreiser demands to be read as a cosmic and visionary poet. We do him no honor by referring patronizingly to his "raw bulk" and "savage power," as if he were a primitive writer unschooled in the ways of art. Dreiser's skillful use of documentation in *An American Tragedy* depends precisely on his rich experience of both life and art and on his power to give that experience new life through all of the artistic resources at his command.

An American Tragedy is not a reproduction of literal reality, but, drawn from real life experience, it heightens and intensifies our understanding of reality. Dreiser's art comes closer than that of perhaps any other major novelist of our time to breaking down the antithesis between life and art. His illumination of the human condition is through an art that on occasion is so close to reality as to threaten to blur the separation of the fictive and the real. To the extent that Dreiser is an artist, *An American Tragedy* transcends the documentary and the purely historical; without its documentary foundations, however, the novel could not have exercised its hold on Dreiser's imagination. *An American Tragedy* asserts the strength of the novelist to confront large questions, to range boldly over a wide arc of life, and to penetrate below the surface of experience to the underlying instinctive and social forces and motives that shape human destiny. For this exploration, Dreiser had a rare honesty and courage and enough art for his task.

V
Conclusion: The Fictive and the Real

The dynamic interplay of the fictive and the real in the three naturalistic novels that we have studied demonstrates conclusively the inventive power of their creators. It can be cogently argued that *L'Assommoir, Buddenbrooks,* and *An American Tragedy* are their authors' finest fictional achievements. If few other naturalistic novels attain so high a quality of artistic expression, we should not thereby condemn naturalism itself; a style should be judged by its best examples, not by its worst. No other novels by Zola, Mann, or Dreiser dramatize more strikingly the tensions between life and art. None of these novels, nor any other novel of high artistic merit, conforms absolutely to the theoretical requirements for the naturalistic novel set forth by Zola; yet, with all due allowance for the variety of styles present in each novel, all three are distinctly naturalistic. All depend to a considerable extent on the accurate and literal observation of reality; all purport to present human experience honestly and convincingly; and all reflect a deterministic view of events that is derived from the natural sciences and represented in the operation of biological and social forces. The mere presence, however, of naturalistic techniques and values in a novel tells us nothing about the artistry with which they are expressed. This artistry is always contextual; it depends squarely on what the novelist makes out of his resources. The novels of Zola, Mann, and Dreiser that we have examined are unmistakable proof of the imaginative power naturalistic fiction possesses at its highest reach.

The complexities of the interrelationship of fiction and reality are, of course, not peculiar to the naturalistic novel. The fundamental problem of the naturalists is as old as the classical problem of mimesis: How does the artist represent reality, or more precisely, how does the work of art imitate or represent real experience? Of all literary forms, the novel from its very inception has been the closest to the surface of literal events. All novels, as in a broad sense all works of art, are concerned with the interplay of the fictive and the real. Documentation did not begin with the naturalists, nor did it end with them. It is a possible mode of procedure for any novelist, naturalistic or not. More than most novelists, however, the naturalists, in their emphasis on truthfulness to actuality and on the role of documentation in the process of composition, run the risk of blurring the distinction between undifferentiated and inchoate life and the selection and arrangement of art. The objective and literal transcription of everyday events is at the farthest possible remove from the intensity and monumentality of great art. The allegedly scientific method of Zola and his followers is repudiated on virtually every page of their novels. Were this not the case, their works would be incapable of engaging us as they do and of enlarging our understanding of both life and art. Zola, Mann, and Dreiser all speak to us, each in his own way, as authentic poets, establishing through the power of art their sovereignty over the kingdom of the imagination.

The naturalistic novelist is therefore both like and unlike his predecessors. After the Romantics had widened the gap between fiction and reality and after an ever-growing number of purveyors of short-run and idle entertainment had trivialized the novel, the naturalists, while narrowing the distance that separates life and art, reinvested the novel with dignity and human pertinence. Their preoccupation with the sordid and mean, with disease, decay, and death, and their conscious effort to expand the subject matter and language of the novel broke new ground in a bold and arresting way. Not that previous novelists had wholly neglected the area that the naturalists claimed as their own—Dickens, Flaubert, and Dostoevsky present scenes of human misery and squalor which vie with those of any of the novels we have discussed—but the naturalistic novelist, in his probing obsession with the operative force of the milieu, confronted more immediately than did his predecessors the social processes and institutions that he saw as responsible for the fate of his characters and of their counterparts in real life.

The honesty and force of naturalistic fiction shocked and infuriated contemporary readers in a way that we may find difficult to understand today. It seems incredible that the poet Swinburne, in a letter of July 11, 1879, could have called *L'Assommoir* "the most horrible and loathsome book that ever got into type" and that Henry James, in a review of *Nana* published in *The Parisian* in 1880 and reprinted by Cornelia P. Kelley, could have complained of "that ferociously bad smell which blows through *L'Assommoir* like an emanation from an open drain," even though he praised the novel's "magnificent passages and episodes." Far worse than these typical expressions of the criticism of the day was the imprisonment for three months in 1889 of Zola's English publisher, Henry Vizetelly, solely for publishing translations of Zola that had already been expurgated in the hope of complying with the law. To be sure, writers and publishers have suffered far more severe punishments in other times and places; but the episode is no less outrageous simply because the publisher's fate might have been worse. The imprisonment serves to point up the urgency of the campaign that Zola and his followers waged to widen the boundaries of the novel and bring it into nearer accord with the realities of modern life.

The naturalists share in the great tradition of the novelist as social historian of both past and present. Zola's *Rougon-Macquart* is at once a history of a family and of a whole society. In George Moore's *A Modern Lover* (1883), the novelist Harding, an author of allegedly immoral and cynical fiction, speaks for Moore and for all naturalistic novelists when he says: "The novel, if it be anything, is contemporary history, an exact and complete reproduction of social surroundings of the age we live in." The naturalists did not invent this conception of the novel, but they gave it new emphasis and relevance at a time when this was badly needed. The depiction of social processes and events in their best fiction is not a mere transcription of reality. The naturalistic novelist goes well beyond the simple chronicler of events in his use of the novel as a means of diagnosing the causes of human ills and of pointing to a remedy for them, when remedies are possible. Documentation plays a vital role in this process, for it enables the naturalistic novelist to provide convincing assurance, within the precincts of his novel, that the experiences he presents are true to life. Here again, he joins hands with a long tradition of confreres. From the very beginnings of the novel as an art form, its practitioners have drawn directly on their own experiences and have appealed to the truthfulness of their narrative by way of defending the novel from attack as a trivial or dangerous pursuit. Truth has always served as an apology for fiction of every kind and quality; but the greatest of novels impose their authenticity through the intrinsic values of their art. For the naturalists, the canon of truth implies a fictional art that represents honestly and uncompromisingly the circumstances and events of actual experience.

Zola, Mann, and Dreiser are all powerful novelists. Their best novels not only correspond to our sense of reality; they illuminate and heighten our understanding of the world around us. This intensified realism is in large measure a direct consequence of their selective and purposeful documentation. The study of their processes of documentation—its sources, its modes of employment, and its role in fictional creation—can help us better understand the distinctive qualities of the naturalistic novel as a fictional style. On the basis of our examination of the processes of composition in *L'Assommoir, Buddenbrooks,* and *An American Tragedy,* we can suggest at least tentative generalizations concerning the relationship of fiction to reality in the naturalistic novel. Yet any such generalizations, even if based on a much wider range of examples, are bound to be only statements of probability that are necessarily incomplete and incapable of absolute verification. We can never know all of the sources of a work of art, for these are never solely literary or documentary in origin. It is precisely because of the complex nature of the creative process that studies of literary origins or influences are of such limited value as explanations of the character of a work of art. The novelist, like the painter and the poet, may draw on any area of experience in the shaping of his art. Moreover, our knowledge of the precise activity of the artist in his workshop is most imperfect. Even after considerable documentary material has been brought to light, we seldom know what choices the novelist had to make and what alternatives he considered in the act of composition. Investigations of the origins of a work of art and their role in its composition must always begin with the work itself as a point of departure. As art, the finished work can never stand in a simple cause and effect relationship to any external source. The materials, so-called, of a novel are inseparable from the novelist's vision of reality and his imaginative power. All novels can be viewed as "documentary" if we define the term with sufficient breadth. It would be naïve, however, to suppose that all novelists, poets, and playwrights must have literally experienced the events portrayed in their art or that their subject matter is limited to what they have actually observed. Documentation is often a starting point for the novelist, but it can never be an end in itself if the novel is to transcend the plane of the documentary. No juxtaposition of a document and a work of art can provide in and of itself a measure of aesthetic value. The most extensive and conscientious documentation can issue in mediocre art or great art, according to the total capacities of the artist.

Great art is by definition in a class by itself. A truly significant novel is stamped with the individuality and artistry of the novelist. No discussion of a common approach to the novel can fail to recognize that the quality of a work of art is defined not simply by the conventions and norms which it shares with other works but by its radical uniqueness. Nevertheless, we can gain in our understanding and appreciation of a novelist's art by setting his novel alongside other novels which may provide mutual illumination. In our study of the novels of Zola, Mann, and Dreiser, we have seen that, although each novelist impressed his personal vision and style upon his work, all three relied extensively on documentation as a source of verisimilitude. All of them were animated by a passion for the exact detail. To be sure, naturalistic theories and techniques can account only partially for their compelling need to engage in deliberate research as a prelude to writing. Moreover, the real and important similarities in their processes of composition do not depend on any direct influence Zola, Mann, or Dreiser may have had on one another. Neither Mann nor Dreiser read Zola until relatively late in their careers, nor do they seem to have read each other; but in the literary world of the turn of the century they could not help acquiring some knowledge of Zola's program, and even if they did not read him, they certainly read other novelists who either anticipated or drew upon Zola's efforts. It is amusing to note in passing that a list of important contemporary German authors compiled by Dreiser in 1911 includes Oswald Bilse but not Thomas Mann. Zola, Mann, and Dreiser did not need to influence one another in order to share common processes of composition. Both by temperament and by conviction, all three novelists were impelled to assimilate the background of their novels as fully as possible, incorporating it into their own experience as a basis for novelistic creation.

Seldom, however, do these novelists employ documentation in their novels merely for its own sake. Almost always, the document is embodied in a larger artistic context in which it ceases to be a document and becomes part of the work of art. The function of the document, thus assimilated and transformed, is always relational. It has independent value as a document only when its artistic integration does not take place, as perhaps in Coupeau's delirium tremens, Hanno's death, and Clyde's trial. Here, documentation is a source of weakness rather than of strength, but such instances are comparatively rare in the novels we have considered.

In all three novels, the use of documentation is highly selective. The passages derived verbatim from an external source are few indeed in proportion to the total fictional expression. The extent as well as the importance of the literal reproduction of documents has been greatly exaggerated in critical appraisals of each of these novels and of naturalistic fiction in general. We have also seen in our examination of characterization that, although Zola, Mann, and Dreiser all drew upon specific models, their characters almost always take on fictional identity with no necessary relation to their supposed counterparts. Just as Tolstoy could declare that, as a fictional character, "Andrei Bolkonsky is nobody," so we can say that, in the same sense, Gervaise or Thomas Buddenbrook or Clyde Griffiths is nobody; they derive their essential being from the pages of their novels. Clearly, at its best, naturalism has nothing to do with so-called photographic realism. The document or the model is only a point of departure, which recedes to the extent that the character is artistically realized. Thomas Buddenbrook is not Senator Thomas Mann but a unique fictional creation.

In general, documentation was a source of strength for Zola, Mann, and Dreiser, stimulating their imaginative powers through suggestion and, at times, leading them far beyond the material at hand. On occasion, it served to remind them of earlier personal experiences, as in Dreiser's incorporation of aspects of his own childhood into that of Clyde Griffiths. Often, the document was merely an *aide-mémoire* or an injunction to the novelist not to lose sight of an aspect of his subject which might otherwise be overlooked in the act of composition. All three novelists drew extensively on their own previous knowledge of the milieu of their novels, supplementing this knowledge through on-the-spot visitations whenever they felt the need to do so. By and large, critics of naturalistic novels have tended to underrate the role of the novelist's prior personal experience and to overstress the importance of his deliberate research into the milieu of the novel, perhaps because the latter is more palpable and more measurable. For Zola, Mann, and Dreiser, the novelist's immersion in the groundwork of his art is essentially a way of asserting his originality. A document, as such, has no absolute authority. We have seen that each of these novelists altered his documentation substantially in order to achieve a specific artistic purpose, as in Tony Buddenbrook's romance with Morten Schwarzkopf and Roberta Alden's drowning. Zola's transformation of the distillation machine is entirely his own. At their best, all three employed documents imaginatively as integral and organic parts of their works.

There does not seem to be any consistent relationship in the naturalistic novel between the minuteness of documentation and the quality of its transformation into art. For although a slight degree of documentary material may stimulate invention, as in Mann's humorous and ironic enlargement of the chance meeting of Tony and Grünlich, and too much documentation may overwhelm even an excellent writer, the determination of "too little" or "too much" can never be made a priori or with certainty but can only be approximated after the fact. All of the novelists we have discussed employed even extensive documentation with considerable latitude. It is clear, however, that they gained far more than they lost through their documentary procedures. By dint of their thorough assimilation of the empirical foundations of their novels, they were able to reassert the rights of authenticity and moral fervor in the face of narrow conventions of the limits and proprieties of fictional expression.

The consequences of naturalism for novelistic form were immense. In each of the novels at hand, documentation encouraged massiveness of composition. This massiveness with its cumulative force reflects the closeness of the novelist to life, especially to those aspects of it—poverty, hereditary disease, sexual immorality, and the like—that were previously regarded as forbidden ground for respectable novelists. In their dominant preoccupation with poverty and vice, the novels of Zola and Dreiser are closer to one another than to *Buddenbrooks,* but all three novels are in the tradition of the large complex plot of the nineteenth century, crammed with incident and defying easy summarization or perusal. Neither hastily composed nor written for readers in a hurry, *L'Assommoir* is substantial enough, whereas the bulk of both *Buddenbrooks* and *An American Tragedy* prompted their publishers to urge Mann and Dreiser to reduce the size of their novels drastically. The novelists did well to refuse, for this massiveness is essential to the impact of their art. We cannot read naturalistic novels in the same way as we would more restricted fiction that is composed according to the view of the novel as a perfect formal construction. The naturalistic novels of Western Europe and America are close in structure to the "loose and baggy monsters," in Henry James' trenchant phrase, of the Russian novel of the mid-nineteenth century. This is not to suggest for a moment that either the Russians or the naturalists neglected structure, but, for the naturalists, the pioneering mission of the novelist and the originality of his vision made other values loom larger and of more immediate import than structure. The structural inadequacies of the naturalistic novel are a reflection of the conflicting claims of the fictive and the real. It must be admitted that the all too solid specification of the naturalistic novel entails both a gain and a loss. A sense of form is not lacking in *L'Assommoir, Buddenbrooks,* and *An American Tragedy,* but the harmony of their parts is not as complete as in novels in which shapeliness of construction is of absolute primacy.

With due allowance for individual differences, in all three of these novels the deterministic premises of naturalism underlie the linking of events and the inevitable movement toward catastrophe. Determinism thus functions not simply as a scientific analogy but as a structural principle. The naturalistic novelist stresses the depiction of the environment out of his belief in a causal relationship between the milieu and the fate of the individual. We feel a similar sense of entrapment in all three novels. Gervaise, Hanno, and Clyde all die harsh deaths as passive victims of a malign fate. Gervaise is the least passive and the most sympathetic of the three, but all of the defeated arouse our compassion if not always our admiration. The novelist's awareness of deterministic processes stimulates not only his pity for the victims of their iron laws but also his indignation over the failure of society to remedy misfortune and suffering. We have seen that it is an easy and a natural transition for the naturalistic novelist to move from documentation to exhortation. To the extent that deterministic forces are subject to amelioration, either by changing society or by controlling the effects of social processes, the naturalistic novelist functions as a moralist and social reformer, as in the angry response of Zola to the death of little Lalie and of Dreiser to death row. The naturalistic novelist's deep human sympathy for the poor and the hungry and his outrage over the squalor of everyday life in the slums of festering cities give continuing relevance to his art in our own day, in an age confronted by the paradox of widespread poverty and desperation amid an abundance of wealth. The tendentiousness of the naturalistic novel invests it with burning moral passion and purposiveness. This tendentiousness is muted and indirect in *Buddenbrooks,* but it is there, as in Mann's account of Hanno's typical school day, marked in virtually every detail by the stupidity and cruelty of the educational system.

The concern with social forces in the naturalistic novel is often at the expense of characterization. A character cannot at once be determined and free. The deprivation of freedom in naturalistic fiction reduces our interest in characters as individuals, even as it heightens their representative function. The most notable exception is Thomas Buddenbrook, for, as a divided and introspective figure, he reflects on his condition and comes to at least a partial understanding of it. His inwardness and ambiguity place him at the center of the decline of the Buddenbrook family and invest him with a complexity that is absent in Gervaise and Clyde. All the same, Thomas Buddenbrook dies a terrible death, and Hanno is brutally sacrificed to the principle of biological determinism. For the victims of determinism, the possibility of an escape from their destiny does not exist. Although Mann, in permitting his characters at least some insight into their condition, thereby reasserts the rights of human intelligence, in *L'Assommoir* and *An American Tragedy* it is the voice of the novelist himself that fills this role. Both Gervaise and Clyde are ultimately reduced to stupefaction and animality, with little or no awareness of the meaning of their experience. It must be added, however, that by making us care about the fate of their principals, Zola and Dreiser invest low and seemingly commonplace characters with dignity and, at times, with nobility. The assertion of the worth of the individual, no matter how lowly, is an implicit qualification of the deterministic premises of naturalistic doctrine. In the novels that we have considered, it is clear that the more mitigated naturalism of Mann makes for far more interesting and more challenging characterization, but it should also be recognized that both Zola and Dreiser portray their central characters as individuals and not simply as case studies or as representatives of their class or of a suppositious "statistical average."

It would be wrong to define naturalism merely by its preoccupation with "low" or impoverished characters. To be sure, Zola and Dreiser, in presenting the condition of the very poor—those at the bottom of the social order—thereby proclaim the artistic value of an area of experience ignored, if not expressly repudiated, by most earlier novelists. The example of *Buddenbrooks* proves, however, that naturalism need not be limited to low and impoverished characters. The Buddenbrooks are a wealthy and prominent family, and they too are helpless victims of inevitable decay. In all three novels the individual experience serves primarily as a mode of broad social generalization; Zola's novel is not *La Simple Vie de Gervaise Macquart* but *L'Assommoir,* and Dreiser's is not *Mirage* but *An American Tragedy. Buddenbrooks* is a collective title of a novel with a collective hero. The determinism of the naturalistic novel transforms the natural and social order to the status of a metaphysical absolute. In a universe without God and in which men are weak and passive victims of destiny, an impersonal milieu becomes the sole center of authority.

To the extent that these novelists humanize their characters and make us enter into their suffering, they militate against the nihilistic implications of a thoroughgoing naturalistic world view. Clearly, neither Zola nor Mann, nor even Dreiser, was absolutely and uncompromisingly naturalistic in his novels. All three novelists assert the promise as well as the failure of life, its joy as well as its pain, its aspiration as well as its defeat. As Thomas Mann rightly contended, to the extent that a work of art engages our minds and hearts, it cannot be nihilistic. Beyond the anguish and despair of the victims of biological and social processes is the hope inherent in a new clarity of vision. The courage of the naturalistic novelists to confront the darkness and bitterness of experience is an act in praise of life and its possibilities, however brutal the reality represented in their novels may be.

It is to the great credit of the naturalistic novelists that, in their best works, they made even sordid and ugly aspects of reality artistic. The expansion of subject matter was accompanied by an expansion of language such as we have seen reflected in *L'Assommoir*. Zola and his followers did not limit their linguistic experimentation to the dialect or slang of lower-class life. They sought instead to give the language of the novel a distinct artistic value. Even in *The Experimental Novel,* in an essay on Goncourt's *Les Frères Zemganno,* Zola urges the young novelists of the day to try to have a style that will be "strong, solid, simple, human," marked by the perfection of the "*mot juste* in its right place." Clearly, Zola learned more from Flaubert than the trenchant anatomy of social manners and values. He shares with Flaubert the aspiration toward an artistic prose that would raise the novel to the power of poetry. George Moore, in *Confessions of a Young Man,* contends that the language of English fiction has "run stagnant" and predicts that if the art of the new realistic novelists should take hold in England, "the English tongue may be saved from dissolution, for with the new subjects they would introduce, new forms of language would arise." The expansion of the linguistic resources of the novel is among Zola's foremost accomplishments. After *L'Assommoir,* even the meanest of subjects could be presented artistically through the imaginative employment of the rhythmic and evocative resources of language.

At its best, the language of naturalistic fiction is richly metaphorical. The artistic prose of Zola and his followers imposes on the language of the novel precisely the same function as the language of poetry. The embodiments of physical reality in their fiction are not mere objects but repositories of symbolic value. Perhaps nowhere is Zola's penchant for the excessive and the gigantic so markedly in evidence as in his bold and strident enlargement of the controlling metaphors of his fiction. The very presence of symbolic and mythic projections points to a fundamental cleavage between Zola's alleged determinism and his art. His poetic distortion and amplification are poles apart from any literal and objective reproduction of reality. The same imaginative departure from the confines of verisimilitude may be seen in Thomas Mann's intricate employment of the leitmotif and in the invocation of dream, phantasmagoria, and nightmare in Dreiser's depiction of the inner torments of Clyde Griffiths. The poetic values of the naturalistic novel are in striking contradiction both to the theories of "The Experimental Novel" and the conventional descriptions of naturalism. Donald Pizer has suggested in *Realism and Naturalism in Nineteenth-Century American Literature* that in our failure to recognize the extraordinary and excessive qualities of their fiction, we have "done a disservice to the late nineteenth-century American naturalists by our earlier simplistic conception of their art." Until very recently, the same simplification affected the understanding of European naturalistic fiction as well, most notably that of Zola. If we read this fiction with the same imaginative sympathy that we may bring to other modes of expression, we cannot escape the conclusion that, at its best, the naturalistic novel attains the intensity and grandeur of high art. Despite the claims of verisimilitude, the rights of the novelist, grounded in the imaginative freedom of his art, are absolute. In truly significant naturalistic novels, the fictive boldly proclaims its authority over the real.

The irresistible pressure of a harsh reality is the hallmark of the naturalistic novel, but, as we have seen, individual novelists appropriate and transform reality in their own way. In the composition of the novels we have studied, both Mann and Dreiser placed considerable weight on factual documentation; yet Mann actually widened the distance between the fictive and the real whereas Dreiser narrowed it. In some degree, Zola, Mann, and Dreiser all recognized a certain distance separating life and art, and all showed at least some theoretical understanding of the problem of their interplay. Zola and Mann, more inclined than Dreiser to engage in controversial exchanges with hostile critics, were also more inclined to speculate on the nature of artistic creation and to develop their reflections in extended critical or philosophical essays. Nevertheless, all three writers are in remarkable agreement on the absolute authority of the novelist in the act of creation. Paradoxically, the freedom that the naturalistic novelists seem to refuse to their characters, they reclaim for themselves. Zola's ringing declaration, "Je prends mes documents où je les trouve, et je crois les faire miens" ("I take my documents wherever I find them, and I think I make them mine"), could have been made with no less vigor and justification by Mann or Dreiser. Their art is simultaneously like life and essentially different from it. It has been all too easy for readers to patronize the naturalists. Most discussions of naturalism have emphasized not its accomplishments but its weaknesses. Increasingly, however, the superficial judgment of conventional criticism is giving way to the recognition of the positive values of naturalistic art: its honesty, imaginative boldness, and deep human pertinence.

At a distance of well over half a century, we need to reevaluate naturalistic fiction, not according to the expressed theories of the novelists, interesting though these might be, but in relation to the fiction itself. The novelists' assertions of doctrine are not wholly irrelevant to our understanding of their novels, but their theories must be derived from their art, as an expression of what Renato Poggioli has called "unwritten poetics." The naturalists' conception of their art is far more imaginative than most descriptions of naturalism would suggest.

We may conclude that naturalistic fiction is fully capable of attaining the intensity and dignity of great art. Nevertheless, the fact that Zola, Mann, and Dreiser wrote naturalistically does not make them great novelists. Naturalism, like any other fictional style, may yield mediocre novels or magnificent ones, depending on the art of the novelist. A style and its techniques are an incentive to a writer, but they acquire their true significance only within the context of his work. We may fittingly describe *L'Assommoir, Buddenbrooks,* and *An American Tragedy* as major naturalistic novels, yet, despite the common principles animating their composition, each writer imposes a distinctly personal artistic vision on his creation. Where Dreiser overwhelms the reader with detail, Mann subtly interrelates themes and images, blending them intricately and artfully into the texture of his work. We do not read Zola for the qualities of Mann, nor do we look for Mann's refined nuances and conscious reflection of a rich cultural tradition in the novels of Dreiser. Nevertheless, the qualities that writers share are at least as important for our understanding of their art as those that differentiate them. As naturalistic novelists, Zola, Mann, and Dreiser offer convincing proof that naturalism and artistic creation are fully compatible, provided that the values and techniques of naturalism are translated into imaginative expression. It is ultimately with poetic receptivity that we must approach the great naturalistic novelists of the turn of the century, and it is as poets that they will continue to be read.

Notes

Chapter I

1. See F. W. J. Hemmings, "The Origin of the Terms *Naturalisme, Naturaliste,*" *French Studies,* 8 (1954), 109–121; also, Guy Robert, *Emile Zola* (Paris, 1952), p. 184, *n.* 19; and René Wellek, *A History of Modern Criticism* (New Haven, 1965), IV, 15.
2. Cited in John C. Lapp, "Taine et Zola: Autour d'une Correspondance," *Revue des Sciences Humaines,* 87 (1957), 321.
3. Edmond and Jules de Goncourt, *Journal* (Paris, 1935), V, 234.
4. Zola, *Documents littéraires* (Paris, 1929), p. 204.
5. Frank Norris, "Zola as a Romantic Writer," in *The Literary Criticism of Frank Norris* (Austin, 1964), pp. 71–72.
6. See Edmondo de Amicis, *Souvenirs de Paris et de Londres* (Paris, 1880), pp. 192–202; Paul Alexis, *Emile Zola* (Paris, 1882), pp. 157–166; F. W. J. Hemmings, *Emile Zola* (Oxford, 1966), pp. 63–68.
7. Henry James, letter of December 12, 1884, to Thomas Sergeant Perry, in Virginia Harlow, *Thomas Sergeant Perry: A Biography* (Durham, N.C., 1950), p. 319.

Chapter II

1. The standard study is Henri Massis, *Comment Emile Zola composait ses romans* (Paris, 1906).
2. See F. W. J. Hemmings, "The Elaboration of Character in the *Ebauches* of Zola's Rougon-Macquart Novels," *PMLA,* 81 (1966), 286.
3. The text is reprinted in Massis, pp. 190–198. The relevant

passages of Louis Ratisbonne's article in *L'Evénement* are reprinted in Massis, pp. 95–96.

4. For a list of the written sources of documentation in *L'Assommoir*, see Emile Zola, *Les Rougon-Macquart*, Bibliothèque de la Pléiade (Paris, 1961), II, 1567–1568.

5. For parallel passages, see Massis, pp. 178–185.

6. Massis, p. 329.

7. Zola, "Lettre au Directeur du *Bien Public*," *Correspondance (1872–1902)* (Paris, 1929), p. 469.

8. Massis, p. 130.

9. Zola, *Correspondance (1872–1902)*, p. 469.

10. See Léon Deffoux, *La Publication de l'Assommoir* (Paris, 1931), p. 43.

11. Cited in Deffoux, p. 112.

12. Reprinted in Zola, *Nouvelle Campagne 1896* (Paris, 1897), pp. 245–260.

13. *Ibid.*, pp. 253–254.

14. See Zola's letter of September 9, 1876, to Albert Millaud, in *Correspondance (1872–1902)*, p. 455.

15. Marcel Cressot, "La Langue de 'l'Assommoir'," *Le Francais moderne*, 8 (1940), 212.

16. Henri Mitterand, "Quelques aspects de la création littéraire dans l'œuvre d'Emile Zola," *Les Cahiers Naturalistes*, 24–25 (1963), 13.

17. Flaubert, *Correspondance* (Paris, 1930), VIII, 19, 25.

18. Erich Auerbach, *Mimesis* (Bern, 1959), p. 478.

19. Thomas Mann, "Fragment über Zola," *Nachlese* (Berlin, 1956), p. 153.

Chapter III

1. Thomas Mann, *Betrachtungen eines Unpolitischen* (Berlin, 1920), p. 53.

2. Thomas Mann, "Lübeck als geistige Lebensform," *Altes und Neues* (Frankfurt am Main, 1953), p. 294.

3. *Ibid.*, p. 298.

4. Thomas Mann, "Zu einem Kapitel aus *Buddenbrooks*," *Altes und Neues*, p. 568.

5. Cited in Alfred Kantorowicz, *Heinrich und Thomas Mann* (Berlin, 1956), p. 76.

6. Paul Scherrer, "Aus Thomas Manns Vorarbeiten zu den *Buddenbrooks,*" *Librarium,* 2 (1959), 127.

7. Cited in Paul Scherrer, "Thomas Mann und die Wirklichkeit," *Lübeckische Blätter,* 120 (April 2, 1960), 78.

8. Heinrich Mann, *Ein Zeitalter wird besichtigt* (Berlin, 1947), pp. 232–233.

9. Julia Mann, "Tante Elisabeth," *Sinn und Form,* 15 (1963), 482–496. Excerpts from Aunt Elisabeth's letter appear in Paul Scherrer, "Aus Thomas Manns Vorarbeiten zu den *Buddenbrooks,*" pp. 22–35; 122–136.

10. Paul Scherrer, "Thomas Mann und die Wirklichkeit," *Lübeckische Blätter,* 120 (April 2, 1960), 78 and Ab. No. 3.

11. See Thomas Mann, *Nachlese,* p. 146, for his insistence on his command of Munich dialect.

12. See Paul Scherrer, "Thomas Manns Mutter liefert Rezepte für die *Buddenbrooks,*" in Christian Voigt and Erich Zimmermann (eds.), *Libris et Litteris: Festschrift für Hermann Tiemann* (Hamburg, 1959), pp. 325–337.

13. Compare the chart of the Mann family in Viktor Mann, *Wir waren Fünf* (Konstanz, 1949), pp. 500–501, with the "Zeittafel der Familiengeschichte der Buddenbrooks," in Hellmuth Petriconi, *Das Reich des Untergangs* (Hamburg, 1958), pp. 191–192.

14. A comparative table of the characters in the novel and their models, prepared by a resident of Lübeck shortly after the publication of *Buddenbrooks,* is reproduced in Klaus Schröter, *Thomas Mann in Selbstzeugnissen und Bilddokumenten* (Reinbek b. Hamburg, 1964), p. 78.

15. I am grateful to the Bibliothek der Hansestadt Lübeck for sending me a copy of this advertisement.

16. Thomas Mann, "Bilse und Ich," *Altes und Neues,* p. 24.

17. Thomas Mann, *Briefe 1889–1936* (Frankfurt am Main, 1961), p. 63.

18. Leo Tolstoy, letter of May 3, 1865, to L. I. Volkonskaya, cited in R. F. Christian, *Tolstoy's* War and Peace (Oxford, 1962), p. 86.

19. The covering letter is reprinted in *Sinn und Form,* 15 (1963), 482, immediately preceding the text of the report.

20. Paul Scherrer, "Aus Thomas Manns Vorarbeiten zu den *Buddenbrooks,*" p. 24.

21. See Eberhard Lämmert, "Thomas Mann: *Buddenbrooks,*" in Benno von Wiese (ed.), *Der Deutsche Roman* (Düsseldorf, 1963), II, 206–210.

22. Rainer Maria Rilke, "Thomas Mann's *Buddenbrooks,*" *Bremer Tageblatt,* April 16, 1902, reprinted in Rilke, *Sämtliche Werke* (Frankfurt am Main, 1965), V, 581.

23. Thomas Mann, *Briefe 1889–1936,* p. 62.

24. Paul Scherrer, "Aus Thomas Manns Vorarbeiten zu den *Buddenbrooks,*" p. 23.

Chapter IV

1. Frank Harris, *Contemporary Portraits: Second Series* (New York, 1919), p. 91. Also see Dreiser's letter of May 13, 1916, in *Letters of Theodore Dreiser: A Selection* (Philadelphia, 1959), I, 211.

2. Cited in W. A. Swanberg, *Dreiser* (New York, 1965), p. 291.

3. Cited in Swanberg, p. 193.

4. Helen Dreiser, *My Life with Dreiser* (Cleveland, 1951), p. 76.

5. Theodore Dreiser, "I Find the Real American Tragedy," *Mystery,* 11 (February 1935), 10–11, 88–90; (March 1935), 22–23, 77–79; (April 1935), 24–26, 90–92; (May 1935), 22–24, 83–86; (June 1935), 20–21; 68–73.

6. For these and other parallels to contemporary newspaper reports, see Emil Greenberg, *A Case Study in the Technique of Realism: Theodore Dreiser's* An American Tragedy (M.A. thesis, New York University, 1936).

7. Oscar Cargill, *Intellectual America* (New York, 1959), p. 111.

8. For resulting complications of this visit, see Dreiser's letter to H. L. Mencken of December 3, 1925, in *Letters of Theodore Dreiser,* II, 435–437.

9. For a comparison of texts, see Greenberg, p. 56.

10. Dreiser's modifications of his sources are ably discussed by Robert H. Elias, *Theodore Dreiser* (New York, 1949), pp. 221–222 and by F. O. Matthiessen, *Theodore Dreiser* (New York, 1951), p. 192. See also Helen Dreiser, p. 76.

11. Theodore Dreiser, "I Find the Real American Tragedy," *Mystery,* 11 (February 1935), 89.

12. Letter of Horace Liveright of May 6, 1924, to Theodore Dreiser, cited in Swanberg, p. 286.

13. Cited in Swanberg, p. 287.
14. For a representative early view of Dreiser as a mere photographer, see Stuart P. Sherman, "The Barbaric Naturalism of Mr. Dreiser," in Alfred Kazin and Charles Shapiro (eds.), *The Stature of Theodore Dreiser* (Bloomington, 1955), p. 74. For a more recent application of this view to *An American Tragedy*, see Randall Stewart, "Dreiser and the Naturalistic Heresy," *Virginia Quarterly Review,* 34 (1958), 100–116.
15. For an illuminating discussion of shifting perspectives in the novel, see Robert Penn Warren, *"An American Tragedy," Yale Review,* 52 (1962), 1–15.
16. Swanberg, p. 294.
17. Cited in Helen Dreiser, p. 77.

Bibliography

General Studies

Ahnebrink, Lars. *The Beginning of Naturalism in American Fiction.* Uppsala, Sweden: Almqvist and Wiksell, 1950.

Becker, George J. (ed.). *Documents of Modern Literary Realism.* Princeton: Princeton University Press, 1963.

Beuchat, Charles. *Histoire du naturalisme français.* 2 vols. Paris: Correa, 1949.

Brunetière, Ferdinand. *Le Roman naturaliste.* Paris: Calmann Lévy, 1892.

Charlton, D. G. *Positivist Thought in France during the Second Empire, 1852–1870.* Oxford: The Clarendon Press, 1959.

Cogny, Pierre. *Le Naturalisme.* Paris: Presses Universitaires de France, 1959.

Cowley, Malcolm. "Naturalism in American Literature," in Stow Persons (ed.), *Evolutionary Thought in America.* New Haven: Yale University Press, 1950. Pp. 299–333.

Deffoux, Léon. *Le Naturalisme.* Paris: Les Œuvres représentatives, 1929.

Desprez, Louis. *L'Evolution naturaliste.* Paris: Tresse, 1884.

Frierson, William C. *The English Novel in Transition, 1885–1940.* Norman: University of Oklahoma Press, 1942.

Hamann, Richard, and Jost Hermand. *Naturalismus.* Berlin: Akademie Verlag, 1959.

Hemmings, F. W. J. "The Origin of the Terms *Naturalisme, Naturaliste,*" *French Studies,* 8 (1954), 109–121.

Martino, Pierre. *Le Naturalisme français.* Paris: Colin, 1923.

Pizer, Donald. *Realism and Naturalism in Nineteenth-Century Amer-*

ican Literature. Carbondale: Southern Illinois University Press, 1966.

Poggioli, Renato. "Poetics and Metrics," in Werner P. Friederich (ed.), *Comparative Literature*. Chapel Hill: University of North Carolina Press, 1959. I, 192–204.

Ruprecht, Erich (ed.). *Literarische Manifeste des Naturalismus*. Stuttgart: Metzler, 1962.

Saveson, Marilyn B. *The Influence of Emile Zola upon the Theory and Practice of Some English Novelists of His Time*. Doctoral dissertation, University of Cambridge, 1955.

Wais, Kurt. "Zur Auswirkung des französischen naturalistischen Romans in Deutschland," *An der Grenzen der National-literaturen*. Berlin: de Gruyter, 1958, pp. 215–236.

Walcutt, Charles Child. *American Literary Naturalism, a Divided Stream*. Minneapolis: University of Minnesota Press, 1956.

Wellek, René. *A History of Modern Criticism*. New Haven: Yale University Press, 1965. Vol. IV.

Emile Zola

Zola, Emile. *L'Assommoir*. Paris: Le Club français du livre, 1954.

———. *L'Assommoir*. Atwood H. Townsend (tr.). New York: New American Library, 1962.

———. *Une Campagne*. Paris: Bernouard, 1928.

———. *Correspondance (1872–1902)*. Paris: Bernouard, 1929.

———. *Documents littéraires*. Paris: Bernouard, 1929.

———. *Le Naturalisme au théâtre*. Paris: Charpentier, 1881.

———. *Nouvelle Campagne 1896*. Paris: Fasquelle, 1897.

———. Préface, William Busnach and Octave Gastineau. *L'Assommoir*. Paris: Charpentier, 1901, pp. 7–40.

———. *Le Roman expérimental*. Paris: Bernouard, 1929.

———. *Les Romanciers naturalistes*. Paris: Charpentier, 1881.

———. *Les Rougon-Macquart*. Paris: Gallimard, 1961. Vol. II.

———. *Thérèse Raquin*. Paris: Bernouard, 1929.

———. *Thérèse Raquin*. Willard R. Trask (tr.). New York: Bantam, 1960.

Albérès, R. M. "Que révèle *L'Assommoir* en 1967?" *Revue de Paris,* 74 (février 1967), 51–59.

Alexis, Paul. *Emile Zola: notes d'un ami.* Paris: Charpentier, 1882.

Amicis, Edmondo de. *Souvenirs de Paris et de Londres.* Paris: Hachette, 1880.

Auerbach, Erich. *Mimesis.* Bern: Francke, 1959.

Baldick, Robert. "Zola the Poet," *The Listener,* 54 (December 8, 1955), 992–993.

Bernard, Marc. "Emile Zola et son époque," *Cahiers français d'information,* 213 (1er octobre 1952), 18–19.

Brandes, Georg. "Emile Zola," *Deutsche Rundschau,* 54 (1888), 27–44.

Brown, Calvin S. *Repetition in Zola's Novels.* Athens, Georgia: University of Georgia Press, 1952.

Burns, Colin. "Documentation et imagination chez Emile Zola," *Les Cahiers Naturalistes,* 24–25 (1963), 69–78.

Busnach, William, and Octave Gastineau. *L'Assommoir.* Paris: Charpentier, 1901.

Butor, Michel. "Emile Zola romancier expérimental et la flamme bleue," *Critique,* 23 (1967), 407–437.

Cressot, Marcel. "La langue de *l'Assommoir,*" *Le Français moderne,* 8 (1940), 207–218.

Deffoux, Léon. *La Publication de* l'Assommoir. Paris: Malfère, 1931.

Dubois, Jacques. "Les refuges de Gervaise: Pour un décor symbolique de *l'Assommoir,*" *Les Cahiers Naturalistes,* 30 (1965), 105–117.

Ellis, Havelock. "Zola," in *Affirmations.* London: Constable, 1922, pp. 131–157.

Flaubert, Gustave. *Correspondance.* Paris: Conard, 1930. Vol. VIII.

Gide, André. *Journal, 1888–1939.* Paris: Gallimard, 1948.

———. *Journal.* Justin O'Brien (ed.). New York: Vintage Books, 1956.

Girard, Marcel. "Positions politiques d'Emile Zola jusqu'à l'affaire Dreyfus," *Revue française de science politique,* 5 (1955), 503–528.

————. "Situation d'Emile Zola," *Revue des Sciences Humaines,* 66 (avril-juin, 1952), 137–156.

————. "Zola Visionnaire," *Montjoie,* 1 (Autumn, 1953), 6–9.

Goncourt, Edmond and Jules de. *Journal.* Paris: Fasquelle, 1935. Vol. V.

Grant, Elliott M. *Emile Zola.* New York: Twayne, 1966.

————. *Zola's "Germinal."* Leicester: Leicester University Press, 1962.

Guillemin, Henri. *Présentation des Rougon-Macquart.* Paris: Gallimard, 1964.

Harlow, Virginia. *Thomas Sergeant Perry: A Biography.* Durham, N.C.: Duke University Press, 1950.

Harneit, Rudolf. "Eine ideale Liebe in einem naturalistischen Roman: zur Gestalt des Goujet in Zolas *Assommoir,*" in *Aufsätze zur Themen und Motivgeschichte: Festschrift für Hellmuth Petriconi.* Hamburg: Cram, de Gruyter, 1965. Pp. 151–170.

Hemmings, F. W. J. *Emile Zola.* Oxford: The Clarendon Press, 1966.

————. "The Elaboration of Character in the *Ebauches* of Zola's Rougon-Macquart Novels," *PMLA,* 81 (1966), 286–296.

————. "The Present Position in Zola Studies," *French Studies,* 10 (1956), 97–122.

Henriot, Emile. *Courrier Littéraire XIXe Siècle: Réalistes et Naturalistes.* Paris: A. Michel, 1954.

Huysmans, J.-K. "Emile Zola et *L'Assommoir,*" *En Marge.* Paris: Lesage, 1927. Pp. 7–40.

James, Henry. "Emile Zola," in *Notes on Novelists.* London: Dent, 1914. Pp. 20–50.

Keins, Jean Paul. "Der historische Wahrheitsgehalt in den Romanen Zolas," *Romanische Forschungen,* 46 (1932), 361–396.

Kelley, Cornelia Pulsifer. "Henry James on Zola," *Colby Library Quarterly,* 1 (1943), 46–51.

Kranowski, Nathan. *Paris dans les romans d'Emile Zola.* Paris: Presses Universitaires de France, 1968.

Lanoux, Armand. Introduction to Zola's *L'Assommoir.* Paris: Le Club français du livre, 1954. Pp. i–xxvii.

Lapp, John C. "Taine et Zola: Autour d'une Correspondance," *Revue des Sciences Humaines,* 87 (1957), 319–326.

―――. *Zola before the Rougon-Macquart.* Toronto: University of Toronto Press, 1964.

Le Blond, Maurice. "Notes et Commentaires sur *L'Assommoir,*" in Zola, *L'Assommoir.* Paris: Bernouard, 1928. Pp. 461–496.

Lemaître, Jules. "Emile Zola," in *Les Contemporains.* Paris: Lecène et Oudin, 1887. I, 249–284.

Lepelletier, Edmond. *Emile Zola.* Paris: Mercure de France, 1908.

Leroy, Maxime. "Le prolétariat vu par Zola dans *L'Assommoir,*" *Preuves,* 20 (octobre, 1952), 72–75.

Levin, Harry. *The Gates of Horn: a Study of Five French Realists.* New York: Oxford University Press, 1963.

Lilly, W. S. "The New Naturalism," *Fortnightly Review,* N.S. 38 (1885), 240–256.

Lote, Georges. "Zola historien du Second Empire," *Revue des Etudes Napoléoniennes,* 14 (1918), 39–87.

Lukács, Georg. "Zum hundertsten Geburtstag Zolas," *Der historische Roman.* Neuwied und Berlin: Luchterhand, 1965. Pp. 510–521.

Magnan, Valentin. *De l'Alcoolisme: des diverses formes du délire alcoolique et de leur traitement.* Paris: Delahaye, 1874.

Mallarmé, Stéphane. *Correspondance.* Paris: Gallimard, 1965. Vol. II.

Mann, Thomas. *Nachlese.* Berlin: Fischer, 1956.

Massis, Henri. *Comment Emile Zola composait ses romans.* Paris: Fasquelle, 1906.

Matthews, J. H. *Les Deux Zola.* Genève: Droz, 1957.

Maupassant, Guy de. "Romanciers Contemporains: M. Emile Zola," *Revue Politique et Littéraire,* 31 (1883), 289–294.

Mitterand, Henri. "*L'Assommoir:* Notice," in Zola, *Les Rougon-Macquart.* Paris: Gallimard, 1961. II, 1532–1566.

―――. "Quelques aspects de la création littéraire dans l'œuvre d'Emile Zola," *Les Cahiers Naturalistes,* 24–25 (1963), 9–20.

Moore, George. *Confessions of a Young Man.* London: Laurie, 1904.

―――. *A Modern Lover.* London: Vizetelly, 1885.

————. Preface to Emile Zola, *Piping-Hot!* London: Vizetelly, 1885.

————. Preface to Emile Zola, *The Rush for the Spoil.* London: Vizetelly, 1886.

Nicholas, Brian. "The Novel as Social Document: *L'Assommoir,*" in Ian Gregor and Brian Nicholas, *The Moral and the Story.* London: Faber and Faber, 1962. Pp. 63–97.

Norris, Frank. *The Literary Criticism of Frank Norris.* Donald Pizer (ed.). Austin: University of Texas Press, 1964.

Picon, Gaétan. "Le 'réalisme' d'Emile Zola: du 'tel quel à l'œuvre-objet,' " *Les Cahiers Naturalistes,* 22 (1962), 235–240.

Pommier, Jean. "Les servitudes de l'esprit," in *Conférences de Franz Cumont et de Jean Pommier.* Paris: Droz, 1945. Pp. 83–119.

Poulot, Denis. *Question Sociale: Le Sublime, ou Le Travailleur: comme il est en 1870 et ce qu'il peut être.* Paris: Lecroix, Verboeckhoven, 1870.

Présence de Zola. Paris: Fasquelle, 1953.

Proulx, Alfred C. *Aspects épiques des Rougon-Macquart de Zola.* The Hague: Mouton, 1966.

Robert, Guy. "Le document au service de la création poétique," in *Présence de Zola,* pp. 179–182.

————. *Emile Zola.* Paris: Les Belles Lettres, 1952.

————. *La Terre d'Emile Zola.* Paris: Les Belles Lettres, 1952.

————. (ed.). *Lettres inédites de Louis Desprez à Emile Zola.* Paris: Les Belles Lettres, 1952.

Sanctis, Francesco de. "Studio sopra Emilio Zola," *Nuovi saggi critici.* Napoli: Morano, 1879. Pp. 359–405.

————. "Zola e *L'Assommoir,*" in *Opere.* Milano e Napoli: Ricciardi, 1961, pp. 1067–1090.

————. *Scritti varii inediti o rari.* Napoli: Morano, 1898. Vol. II.

Seccombe, Thomas. "Henry Vizetelly," *Dictionary of National Biography.* London: Smith, Elder, 1909. XX, 385–386.

Swinburne, Algernon Charles. "Note on a Question of the Hour," *The Athenaeum,* June 16, 1877, p. 768.

————. *The Swinburne Letters.* New Haven: Yale University Press, 1960. Vol. IV.

Symonds, John Addington. *"La Bête Humaine.* A Study in Zola's Idealism," *Fortnightly Review,* N.S. 50 (1891), 453–462.

Thibaudet, Albert. "Réflexions: Sur Zola," *Nouvelle Revue Française,* 45 (1935), 906–912.

Turnell, Martin. *The Art of French Fiction.* London: Hamish Hamilton, 1959.

Verhaeren, Emile. "Enquête sur Emile Zola," *La Plume,* 14 (octobre 15, 1902), 1221–1222.

Vissière, Jean-Louis. "L'art de la phrase dans *L'Assommoir,"* *Les Cahiers Naturalistes,* 11 (1958), 455–464.

Walker, Philip D. "Prophetic Myths in Zola," *PMLA,* 74 (1959), 444–452.

Walter, Gerhard. *Emile Zola.* München: Hueber, 1959.

Wenger, Jared. "The Art of the Flashlight: Violent Technique in *Les Rougon-Macquart,"* *PMLA,* 57 (1942), 1137–1159.

Wilson, Angus. *Emile Zola.* London: Secker and Warburg, 1952.

Zévaès, Alexandre. *Zola.* Paris: Editions de la Nouvelle Revue Critique, 1945.

Thomas Mann

Mann, Thomas. *Altes und Neues.* Frankfurt am Main: Fischer, 1953.

————. *Betrachtungen eines Unpolitischen.* Berlin: Fischer, 1920.

————. *Briefe 1889–1936.* Frankfurt am Main: Fischer, 1961.

————. *Buddenbrooks.* 2 vols. Berlin: Fischer, 1914.

————. *Buddenbrooks.* H. T. Lowe-Porter (tr.). New York: Vintage Books, 1952.

————. "Lebensabriss," *Die Neue Rundschau,* 41 (1930), 732–769.

————. *A Sketch of My Life.* H. T. Lowe-Porter (tr.). New York: Knopf, 1960.

————. "Vorwart zu einer Schallplattenausgabe der 'Buddenbrooks,'" *Gesammelte Werke.* Frankfurt am Main: Fischer, 1960. XI, 549–552.

Alberts, Wilhelm. *Thomas Mann und sein Beruf.* Leipzig: Xenien, 1913.

106 / NATURALISTIC TRIPTYCH

Berendsohn, Walter A. "Thomas Manns frühe Meisterschaft," in *Festgabe für L. L. Hammerich*. Copenhagen: Naturmetodens Sproginstitut, 1962. Pp. 1–6.

Bertram, Ernst. "Das Problem des Verfalls," *Mitteilungen der Literarhistorischen Gesellschaft Bonn*, 2 (1907), 72–79.

Christian, R. F. *Tolstoy's* War and Peace. Oxford: Oxford University Press, 1962.

Claus, Horst. *Studien zur Geschichte des deutschen Frühnaturalismus*. Halle: Akademie Verlag, 1933.

Dietzel, Ulrich. "Tony Buddenbrook–Elisabeth Mann: Ein Beitrag zur Werkgeschichte der 'Buddenbrooks,' " *Sinn und Form*, 15 (1963), 497–502.

"Dokumente zur Geschichte der Familie Mann," *Sinn und Form*. Sonderheft Thomas Mann. Berlin, 1965, pp. 10–60.

Eloesser, Arthur. *Thomas Mann, sein Leben und sein Werk*. Berlin: Fischer, 1925.

Freund, Michael. "Herr Permaneder," *Die Gegenwart*, 7 (Dezember 20, 1952), 846–847.

Gronicka, André von. "Thomas Mann and Russia," *Germanic Review*, 20 (1945), 105–137.

Grüters, Walter. *Der Einfluss der norwegischen Literatur auf Thomas Manns "Buddenbrooks"*. Düsseldorf: Triltsch, 1961.

Günther, Irmgard. *Die Einwirkung des skandinavischen Romans auf den deutschen Naturalismus*. Bamberg, 1934.

Hatfield, Henry. *Thomas Mann*. Norfolk, Conn.: New Directions, 1951.

Helbling, Carl. *Thomas Mann und der Naturalismus*. Bern: Grethlein, 1922.

Heller, Erich. *The Ironic German: A Study of Thomas Mann*. London: Secker and Warburg, 1958.

Henze, Eberhard. "Die Rolle des fiktiven Erzählers bei Thomas Mann," *Die Neue Rundschau*, 76 (1965), 189–201.

Hofman, Alois. "Tolstois und Turgenjews humanistischer Realismus in den 'Buddenbrooks,' " *Sinn und Form*. Sonderheft Thomas Mann. Berlin, 1965, pp. 186–203.

Kamnitzer, Heinz. "Buddenbrooks: Bemerkungen zu Zeit und Roman," *Aufbau*, 14 (1958), 582–596.

Kantorowicz, Alfred. *Heinrich und Thomas Mann*. Berlin: Aufbau Verlag, 1956.

Kayser, Wolfgang. *Die Vortragsreise*. Bern: Francke, 1958.

Kuczynski, Jürgen. *Zur westdeutschen Historiographie*. Berlin: Akademie Verlag, 1966.

Lämmert, Eberhard. "Thomas Mann: *Buddenbrooks*," in Benno von Wiese (ed.). *Der Deutsche Roman*. Düsseldorf: Bagel, 1963. II, 190–233.

Lion, Ferdinand. *Thomas Mann*. Zürich: Oprecht, 1947.

Lublinski, Samuel. *Die Bilanz der Moderne*. Berlin: Cronbach, 1904.

Lukács, Georg. *Essays on Thomas Mann*. London: Merlin Press, 1964.

Mann, Heinrich. *Ein Zeitalter wird besichtigt*. Berlin: Aufbau Verlag, 1947.

Mann, Julia. "Tante Elisabeth," *Sinn und Form*, 15 (1963), 482–496.

Mann, Viktor. *Wir waren Fünf*. Konstanz: Südverlag, 1949.

Neider, Charles (ed.). *The Stature of Thomas Mann*. Norfolk, Conn.: New Directions, 1947.

Nivelle, Armand. "La Structure des *Buddenbrooks*," *Revue des Langues Vivantes*, 24 (1958), 323–339.

Pache, Alexander. "*Thomas Manns epische Technik*," *Mitteilungen der Literarhistorischen Gesellschaft Bonn*, 2 (1907), 43–71.

Peacock, Ronald. *Das Leitmotiv bei Thomas Mann*. Bern: Haupt, 1934.

Petriconi, Hellmuth. *Das Reich des Untergangs*. Hamburg: Hoffmann und Campe, 1958.

Rilke, Rainer Maria. *Sämtliche Werke*. Frankfurt am Main: Insel Verlag, 1965. Vol. V.

Royer, Jean. "Lübecker Gotik und Lübecker Strassenbild als Leitmotiv in den 'Buddenbrooks,'" *Nordelbingen*, 33 (1964), 136–150.

Scherrer, Paul. "Aus Thomas Manns Vorarbeiten zu den Buddenbrooks," *Librarium*, 2 (1959), 22–35, 123–136.

————. "Bruchstücke der Buddenbrooks-Urhandschrift und Zeugnisse zu ihrer Entstehung 1897–1901," *Die Neue Rundschau,* 69 (1958), 258–291, 381–382.

————. "Thomas Mann und die Wirklichkeit." *Lübeckische Blätter,* 120 (April 2, 1960), 77–86.

————. "Thomas Manns Mutter liefert Rezepte für die 'Buddenbrooks,' " in Christian Voigt and Erich Zimmermann (eds.), *Libris et Litteris: Festschrift für Hermann Tiemann.* Hamburg: Maximilian, 1959. Pp. 325–337.

Schröter, Klaus. *Thomas Mann in Selbstzeugnissen und Bilddokumenten.* Reinbek bei Hamburg: Rowohlt, 1964.

Sinn und Form. Sonderheft Thomas Mann. Berlin: 1965.

Stresau, Hermann. "Die Buddenbrooks," *Die Neue Rundschau,* 66 (1955), 392–410.

Vajda, György Mihály. "Thomas Mann und das Erbe des neunzehnten Jahrhunderts," in Köpeczi, Béla, and Péter Juhász (eds.). *Littérature et Réalité.* Budapest: Akadémiai Kiadó, 1966. Pp. 191–203.

Theodore Dreiser

Dreiser, Theodore. *An American Tragedy.* Cleveland: World Publishing, 1953.

————. "Background for *An American Tragedy,*" *Esquire,* 50 (October 1958), 155–157.

————. Foreword to Oswald Bilse, *Life in a Garrison Town.* New York: John Lane, 1914. Pp. v–xiii.

————. "I Find the Real American Tragedy," *Mystery,* 11 (February 1935), 10–11, 88–90; (March 1935), 22–23, 77–79; (April 1935), 24–26, 90–92; (May 1935), 22–24, 83–86; (June 1935), 20–21, 68–73.

————. *Letters of Theodore Dreiser: A Selection.* 3 vols. Philadelphia: University of Pennsylvania Press, 1959.

Binni, Francesco. "Dreiser oltre il naturalismo," *Studi Americani,* 11 (1965), 251–269.

Cargill, Oscar. *Intellectual America.* New York: Macmillan, 1959.

Dreiser, Helen. *My Life with Dreiser.* Cleveland: World Publishing, 1951.

Dudley, Dorothy. *Dreiser and the Land of the Free.* New York: Beechhurst Press, 1946.

Elias, Robert H. *Theodore Dreiser.* New York: Knopf, 1949.

Geismar, Maxwell. *Rebels and Ancestors.* Boston: Houghton, Mifflin, 1953.

Gerber, Philip L. *Theodore Dreiser.* New York: Twayne, 1964.

Greenberg. Emil. *A Case Study in the Technique of Realism: Theodore Dreiser's* An American Tragedy. M.A. thesis, New York University, 1936.

Hakutani, Yoshinobu. "Dreiser and French Realism," *Texas Studies in Literature and Language,* 6 (1964), 200–212.

————. "*Sister Carrie* and the Problem of Literary Naturalism," *Twentieth Century Literature,* 13 (1967), 3–17.

Harris, Frank. *Contemporary Portraits: Second Series.* New York: Frank Harris, 1919.

Kazin, Alfred, and Charles Shapiro (eds.). *The Stature of Theodore Dreiser.* Bloomington: Indiana University Press, 1955.

Krutch, Joseph Wood. "Crime and Punishment," *The Nation,* 122 (February 10, 1926), 152.

Lehan, Richard. "Dreiser's *An American Tragedy,*" *College English,* 25 (1963), 187–193.

Matthiessen, F. O. *Theodore Dreiser.* New York: William Morrow, 1951.

Michaud, Régis. *The American Novel Today.* Boston: Little, Brown, 1928.

Parrington, V. L. *Main Currents in American Thought.* New York: Harcourt, Brace & World, 1958.

Shapiro, Charles. *Theodore Dreiser: Our Bitter Patriot.* Carbondale: Southern Illinois University Press, 1962.

Sherman, Stuart P. "The Barbaric Naturalism of Mr. Dreiser," in Alfred Kazin and Charles Shapiro (eds.), *The Stature of Theodore Dreiser,* pp. 71–80.

Stewart, Randall. "Dreiser and the Naturalistic Heresy," *Virginia Quarterly Review,* 34 (1958), 100–116.

Swanberg, W. A. *Dreiser.* New York: Scribner, 1965.

Trilling, Lionel. "Reality in America," in Alfred Kazin and Charles Shapiro (eds.), *The Stature of Theodore Dreiser*, pp. 132–145.

Vivas, Eliseo. "Dreiser, An Inconsistent Mechanist," in Alfred Kazin and Charles Shapiro (eds.), *The Stature of Theodore Dreiser*, pp. 237–245.

Warren, Robert Penn. *"An American Tragedy," Yale Review*, 52 (1962), 1–15.

Index

About the Author

Haskell M. Block is Executive Officer of the Doctoral Program in Comparative Literature of the City University of New York and Professor of Comparative Literature at Brooklyn College. He received his A.B. from the University of Chicago where he was elected to Phi Beta Kappa, his A.M. from Harvard University, and his doctorate from the University of Paris. He has taught at Queens College and the University of Wisconsin, and has served as a visiting professor at the Universities of Hawaii, Illinois, and Colorado, and at Harvard University. He was a Fulbright research scholar at the University of Cologne in 1956–1957 and the University of Paris in 1968–1969.

Professor Block is the author of *Mallarmé and the Symbolist Drama* and of *Nouvelles Tendances en Littérature Comparée*. He has edited and translated Molière's *Tartuffe* and the Modern Library edition of Voltaire, and is co-editor of *The Creative Vision: Modern European Writers on Their Art* and *Masters of Modern Drama*. He is the author of articles on Flaubert, Joyce, Kafka, Camus, and other novelists, and is a frequent contributor to scholarly and critical journals.